HOW
EFFECTIVE
EXECUTIVES
MAKE
STRATEGIC
TIME

GET OUT OF THE WEEDS

Bulk purchase discounts and customized copies are available by contacting the author at https://www.bepioneer.net/

ISBN 978-0-9950905-9-0

This book was published with the support of Happful.com

Dedicated to my family and all others in the pursuit of good ideas.

'Productivity in a day depends on the amount of time you spend doing. Productivity in a year hinges on the amount of time you spend thinking. Productivity in a career rests on the amount of time you spend learning'. - Adam Grant

PREFACE

Getting into the weeds

APPARENTLY, THE PHRASE 'getting into the weeds' has not been with us long. Despite that, it's well known and widely recognized in business to mean two things: a) wandering off your desired path and becoming entangled in too much detail (most of which is irrelevant); and b) becoming overwhelmed.

It's a powerful metaphor for executives because it perfectly describes the situation so many find themselves in. Their primary responsibility is to develop and oversee the implementation of sound organizational strategies, but their ability to do so is constantly compromised because they're 'stuck in the weeds'; entangled in operational concerns.

As hard as they try, they can't make 'strategic time'. Strategic time is time dedicated to strategic priorities; priorities that create maximum organizational and personal value – time that's most meaningful.

This struggle is often overwhelming.

Why I wrote this book

I wrote this book for a number of reasons.

First, I respect executives. They're almost always conscientious, bright, and well-meaning people with a strong desire to do the right thing under challenging circumstances, but most are severely hobbled by a chronic lack of strategic time.

Second, we all have a stake in their success. Organizations affect millions of people, including customers, stakeholders, employees, the public at large, etc. Successful organizations provide the jobs, products, and services we enjoy in life, and boost overall prosperity, while unsuccessful ones do the opposite. Helping executives helps organizations help lots of others.

Finally, I've personally seen a few simple concepts and techniques that help executives who are frustrated and overwhelmed by their inability to get out of the weeds. I hope sharing these concepts and techniques more broadly might help others too.

What's different about this book

I didn't set out to write a time management book as there are loads of them out there, and many are very good. Despite that, I've heard exasperated executives say, 'I can't get out of the weeds' so often, it felt like a different take on the subject was needed.

When I hear executives say they want more time, I hear they want more time out of the weeds; more strategic time. That is the focus of this book.

Executives need more strategic time because the nature of the problems organizations face these days is getting much tougher – this is the focus of Chapter 1.

Executives are responsible for solving the organization's toughest problems, and the new strategic tools and processes necessary for the job demand more strategic time – the focus of Chapter 2.

The effort to make more strategic time should be straightforward, except it typically faces significant personal and organizational barriers – the focus of Chapters 3 and 4. To overcome these barriers, I propose a simple, holistic model that keeps executives focused on all the things they must do to make strategic time - stay out of the weeds – the focus of Chapters 5, 6, 7, 8 and 9.

Despite their best intentions, most executives backslide – the weeds are thick and strong – so a process for diagnosing failure and getting back on track is helpful. This is the focus of Chapter 10.

How to approach this book

One thing I didn't want to do was write a book about strategic time that ended up wasting yours, so I balanced a desire to be comprehensive and direct. You can judge whether I succeeded.

The first four chapters are contextual, laying out the rationale for why making strategic time is such an important and challenging executive priority. These chapters are particularly important for current executives who might question the need to make strategic time, and/or non-executives (high-potential leaders) who aspire to executive positions in future. I hope these early chapters help fuel a powerful intention to get out of the weeds.

However, if you've already resolved to take action and are anxious to get moving, I recommend starting with Chapter 5 (it's short and provides a high-level sense of all the things you must focus on for success). Then go to Chapter 8, 'Create strategic time – pull weeds.' This chapter contains many techniques (low-hanging fruit) to help you make strategic time right now. It's a great starting point if you're buried in the weeds and need a quick intervention.

In Chapter 5, you'll see that I strongly believe the material in Chapters 6 through 9 is critical for sustained success, but Chapter 8 shows you how to take action ASAP and benefit from the motivation and relief that comes from quick wins.

If you want to maintain that initial success, Chapters 1–4 will be a big help. Finally, Chapter 10 will help embed what you've learned in previous chapters as 'good habits', and help you get back on track if (when) you backslide.

At the end of each chapter, you will find a table listing the topics covered in the chapter. If there's a specific topic you want to return to later, circle or make a note next to the page in the table.

CONTENTS

0 Preface v

1 Is there a problem? 1

2 Who is responsible for preventing organizational struggle and failure? 15

3 Why do executives struggle and fail? 33

4 What prevents executives from making and maintaining strategic time? 45

5 How do executives effectively make and maintain strategic time?. 65

6 Allocate strategic time – spot the high ground 77

7 Monitor strategic time – get the lay of the land 103

8 Create strategic time – pull weeds. 115

9 Manage strategic time – prevent weed growth 143

10 Stimulate success and diagnose failure 171

11 Conclusion 187

Thank you 189

References 191

1 IS THERE A PROBLEM?

'If we are going to be part of the solution, we have to engage the problem.' – Meg Whitman

Evidence suggests that there's a big problem

ACCORDING TO THE dictionary, a 'problem' is a situation or matter regarded as unwelcome or harmful and needing to be solved. Evidence suggests that there's a problem (or problems) that makes it much harder for organizations – even very strong ones – to survive, and more importantly, to thrive.

For instance, almost half of the 25 companies included in Tom Peters and Robert Waterman's 1982 book, *In Search of Excellence*, no longer exist, are in bankruptcy or are performing poorly. (1)

In their research into the world's Fortune 1000 companies, the authors of *Built to Change* (2) showed that between 1973 and 1983, the percentage of new companies in the top 20 was 35%. In the subsequent decade the percentage rose to 45% and over the next decade to 60%.

In a 2019 Teradata survey of global leaders, nearly 94% of respondents say they're facing disruption in their industries and are under pressure to rethink approaches and processes to keep pace with market forces.[3] This and other evidence suggests that even our largest, most successful companies are struggling to maintain their competitive position. Struggle and failure is increasing for almost every type of organization, everywhere in the world.

What's causing the increase in organizational struggle and failure?

There are no shortage of opinions – expressed through studies, papers, surveys, etc. – about the problems leading to increased organizational struggle and failure. A review of four references on the matter reveals some common trends.

The top external issues (issues arising outside the organization) for 2019 include increased potential for recession (named twice), trade tariffs and other political instability, cyber security (named twice), competitive risk, supply chain interruption, and changes in legislation and trade.[4][5][6]

Of course these external problems create problems inside organizations, including failing to attract and retain top talent (named twice), creating new business models in response to disruptive technologies, developing next-generation leaders, day-to-day performance pressures, lack of resources, and political turf wars or non-alignment.[4][7]

By extension, these external and internal problems create issues for executives themselves, including managing energy, managing relationships 'up and out', and information flow.[8]

Years ago, I'd recently joined the executive ranks of an organization and met our CEO walking down the corridor. He noticed a worried look on my face and said, 'you look like you've got lots of problems.' I said, 'yes I do.' He said, 'good, otherwise, we don't need you.'

Presented together, this sounds like a lot of problems, but that in itself is not a major cause for concern. After all, executives exist to solve problems like these, and most of you reading this book will be familiar with all of them. Although their relative importance shifts a bit from year to year, many of these problems are the same as those experienced by executives over the last 20 years.

Considering the relative similarity in the types of difficulties executives face over time, is there something about the nature of those problems that's leading to an increase in organizational struggle and failure?

VUCA is the underlying problem

Even though the nature of the problems executives face remains the same, they're getting more difficult to solve than ever before because of rising VUCA.

Four factors dictate the difficulty of a problem:

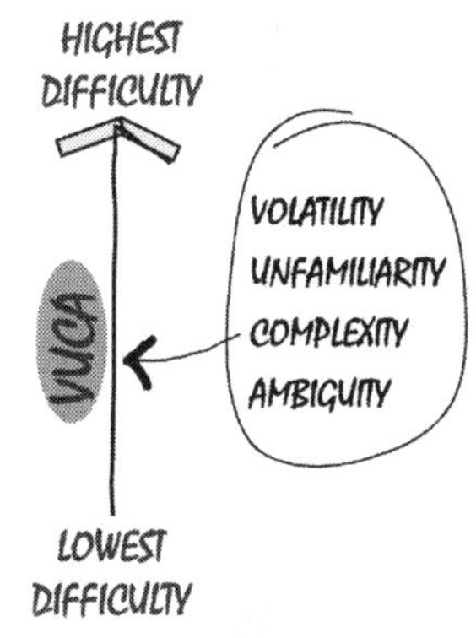

1. Volatility – situations involving big, fast changes are usually more difficult than those with small, slow changes;

2. Unfamiliarity – situations with new, unrecognizable factors are usually more difficult than situations previously encountered and successfully solved;

3. Complexity – situations with indirect and/or hidden interconnections to other situations are usually more difficult than standalone situations; and

4. Ambiguity – situations lacking clarity, exactness, and predictability are usually more difficult than ones with certitude and predictability.

The US Army coined the acronym VUCA to describe how these conditions contribute to disruption and problem-solving difficulties on the battlefield. As volatility, unfamiliarity, complexity, and ambiguity rise in a situation, so do the level of disruption and the difficulty presented by the problem.

Is our organizational environment becoming more disruptive?

Let's consider some quick examples that illustrate how rising volatility, unfamiliarity, complexity, and ambiguity are increasing disruption. Ray Kurzweil [9] writes that our overall rate of progress doubles every 10 years because of technological advances, '...we won't experience 100 years of progress in the 21st century – it will be more like 20,000 years of progress (at today's rate of progress).'

The Future of Employment [10] predicts that within 10 years, around 47% of US companies will be at high risk for technological disruption. According to a World Economic Forum report, [11] 54% of employees in large firms will need to upgrade their skills or acquire entirely new skills.

Hybrid cars have become a common feature on our highways (with autonomous cars being tested in many countries), robotic surgery has become standard for many procedures, music purchased on physical media has become almost obsolete, millions of people now trace their ancestry using mail-order DNA kits, and there are now over three billion smartphones in the world.[12] Remarkably, all these innovations are based on technologies developed within the last 25 years and each has created far-reaching change.

Since his 2016 election, the US president has cancelled or dramatically altered five international agreements or relationships: the North American Free Trade Agreement, the Paris Agreement (climate agreement), the Joint Comprehensive Plan of Action (Iranian nuclear program), the Trans-Pacific Partnership (trade agreement between 12 countries), and instituted steep tariffs on China. Each introduces significant uncertainty and disruption for thousands of organizations.

For a real-life example of the impact rising VUCA and disruption have on organizational struggle and failure, look no further than the 125-year-old (in the US) taxi industry.

Over its entire history, taxi companies have competed with one another, seeking to differentiate themselves on small differences in price and quality of service (and for the last 40 years, the ability to adapt to increasingly heavy regulation).

I've been personally familiar with taxis since the 60s, and for 50 years, little changed – when you wanted a cab you called the dispatcher or hailed one from the curb and waited 10–20 minutes, not knowing when the car would arrive (or whether it would at all).

Typically, your cab driver was a middle-aged man who didn't have a university or college degree. He drove cab for a living, leased or shared his car with someone else, worked 10–14 hours a day, six days a week for a locally owned company and spent as little money as possible maintaining and cleaning a mildly decrepit, mid-aged car. He wanted payment in cash or (reluctantly) with credit card and for all that expected a tip on top of a fare that had been boosted through controls on the supply of taxi licenses.

Then about nine short years ago, Uber launched its first ride-sharing service in San Francisco, and almost everything began to change. Now a phone application hails the car in seconds. You know when it's scheduled to arrive and can easily track its progress.

About 14% of Uber drivers are women (almost twice the industry average),[13] almost half of drivers have a university or college degree, and most don't work full time for anyone (the two biggest reasons drivers join Uber is flexibility and no boss – they work part time).

They typically work two to three hours a day to supplement other income and drive their personal car, which is usually relatively new and in good condition (I've been ferried from the airport to my hotel in a brand-new Tesla twice). In most cities, the fare is about 60% of a traditional cab fare, and payment is automatically charged to your account, with most drivers receiving no tip.

The impact on the taxi industry? Since 2010, Uber and other technology enabled ride-sharing services helped contribute to a 50–60% drop in the value of taxi licenses in many major US cities and a 30% drop in cab rides. Imagine you are a taxi executive (or driver) who started working in 2005. Over a 10-year span, your world was turned upside down.

The taxi industry is certainly not the only industry facing increased VUCA within the past 10–15 years. There are equally compelling examples from the print media, movie, music, and travel industries, among many others. In fact, if your industry has not been significantly disrupted, it's an exception and quite possibly the next-in-line.

Clearly, by any objective measure, VUCA is rising and problem difficulty/disruption is rising with it.

Are organizations prepared for rising VUCA?

Some organizations are much better prepared for rising VUCA than others. For instance, Uber is better prepared for higher VUCA than 99% of their competitors because they're built to create and thrive on disruption – a classic example of a 'Disruptor' or Prospector organization – and traditional cab companies are classic examples of 'Incumbent' or Analyzer and Defender organizations.[14]

The organizational life cycle describes the sequence of stages organizations typically move through as they grow and provides insight into an organization's preparedness for high VUCA.

Though life-cycle models vary, the one I use has five stages:

- Start-Up – an idea is turned into a marketable product and/or service;

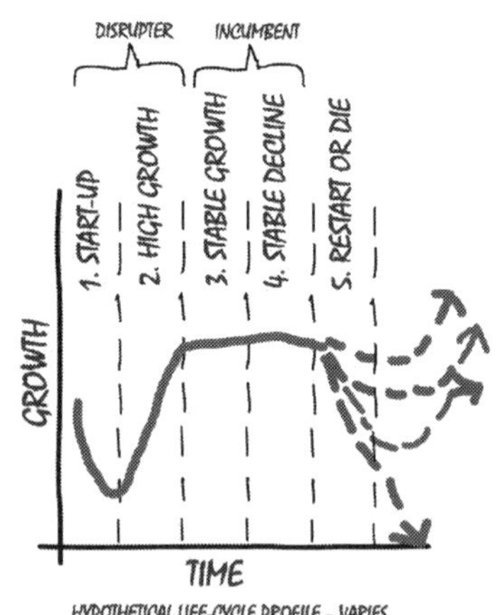

HYPOTHETICAL LIFE-CYCLE PROFILE - VARIES FROM ONE ORGANIZATION TO ANOTHER

- High Growth – high demand for the product/service and growth takes off;
- Stable Growth – growth becomes more incremental;
- Stable Decline – growth declines as demand for product/services lowers; and

- Restart or Die – new product, service and/or market demand is created or the organization slips into decline.

Disruptors combine the development of new products or services, technologies, supply-chain innovations, etc. with speed to gain a foothold in the market – VUCA is their friend because it disrupts markets and incumbents.

Organizations in the first two stages of the life cycle are 'disruptors' and those in the next two are typically 'incumbents.' Incumbents benefit from stability because they control the market. They have relatively large organizations (more people, processes, etc.) and tend to focus internally to squeeze as much value as possible from current products and services in lieu of bold innovations that might cannibalize their current market advantage.

'Companies rarely die from moving too fast and they frequently die from moving too slowly.' Reed Hastings, Netflix

---

It's difficult for incumbents to act like disruptors, especially when their organization has been in Stable Decline for a long period or are unprepared to suddenly face the transition (transformation) to the Restart or Die stage.

Transformation is a daunting task for most incumbents because it means rapid and significant changes to internal policies, processes, systems, and procedures. Worse, the leadership and culture supporting their previous success is relatively unexperienced and unprepared for high VUCA and often reluctant to acknowledge their old business model is in trouble.

Of course, there have always been incumbent organizations traditionally protected from disruption because of regulatory or other barriers to competition, for example monopolies, government, crown-corporations and, to a lesser extent, charitable organizations. However, like traditional cab companies, when they lose their regulatory protection, they're very vulnerable.

Since most organizations are incumbents, most aren't as prepared for a high-VUCA world as they need to be – every incumbent has disruptors trying to steal market share. For instance, a few years ago Deloitte surveyed 700 Canadian business leaders[(15)] to gauge how prepared they were for technological disruption alone, looking at the impact of advanced robotics, artificial intelligence, etc. Only 13% of companies surveyed were fully prepared. Even worse, almost 45% of those surveyed thought they were more prepared than they really were – for them, the threat of disruption is a real and serious blind spot (my experience with the senior teams of many incumbent organizations affirms this – most discount the impact of disruption on their organization until it's too late).

This paints a disturbing picture. VUCA, disruption, and problem difficulty are rising, and most organizations don't feel they're prepared to handle things effectively. It's little wonder levels of organizational struggle and failure are rising and likely to get worse.

Digging deeper into problem difficulty

To provide a better understanding of how rising VUCA is increasing problem difficulty, we need to dig deeper into how problems show up in organizations.

Clearly, all problems aren't created equal. For instance, changing the paper in the photocopier is not as difficult as implementing an Enterprise Resource Package (ERP). Ranging from least to most difficult, we see four different types or levels of problem difficulty in the world – Tame, Complex, Wicked, and Extra Wicked.

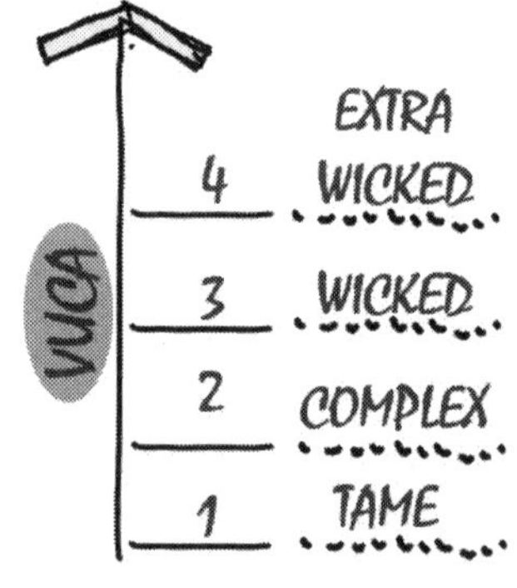

Not every organization experiences all four levels of difficulty. For instance, relatively small organizations – at their highest level of maturity they only have a few employees serving a local market – will likely only ever face Tame problems. However, the largest multi-national organizations, with hundreds of thousands of employees, working across multi-jurisdictional boundaries, face every type of problem, including Extra-Wicked ones.

In between these two extremes you find many organizations – mid to large entities that serve a regional market or larger – that typically face problems ranging between Tame and Wicked levels of difficulty.

To get a sense of how VUCA raises problem difficulty, let's look at our typical progress up the corporate ladder and notice how the nature of the problems we confront change as we elevate.

Tame problems

When we begin our careers, we're usually exclusively focused on Tame problems that share the following characteristics:

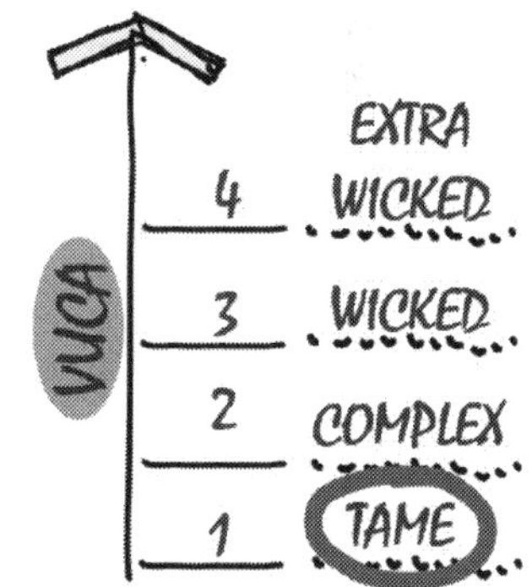

- Low volatility – the situation is relatively stable and changes are so predictable or negligible for the foreseeable future they can be handled by tweaking current processes or procedures;

- Low unfamiliarity – knowledge about how to handle most situations is well known or readily attained through learning or asking someone else for support. In addition, you know how to problem solve effectively with most colleagues because they're familiar to you, similar in age, background, educational experience, and technical/functional area of specialization;

- Low complexity – most situations are relatively discrete, so the ramifications of a bad decision are isolated, limited to your area of work, department, or function; and

- Low ambiguity – the situation is clear, readily understood, and devoid of multiple interpretations, i.e. the time span – the deadline or amount of time it will take to solve the problem – is relatively short, so the path or plan to achieve desired outcomes is easily defined. For example, with most Tame problems you'll likely know a solution works within one year at the most (for many Tame problems, you know whether the solution works almost immediately).

Complex problems

With good performance, we progress through increasingly challenging levels of role and responsibility within our department or function, learning how to tackle increasingly difficult problems until our effectiveness positions us for a role that is more cross-functional or cross-departmental.

As an executive, you know that the characteristics of problems change significantly when we move from a single department role to a multi-departmental one – when we move from Tame to Complex problems – because of:

- Moderate volatility – situations are less stable, changes are bigger and less predictable – a solution to a problem that worked in one department might backfire when applied in another one;

- Moderate unfamiliarity – your knowledge about how to properly diagnose a problem and implement a solution in another department is much lower than in your own. In addition, solving problems as part of a cross-functional group forces you to contend with different perspectives, sources of knowledge, and thinking styles, making collective problem-solving much more challenging;

- Moderate complexity – cross-functional decisions are seldom limited to a discrete part of the business, i.e. a poorly considered policy can impact many other areas in unpredictable ways – the ramifications of a bad decision are much more widespread; and

- Moderate ambiguity – the situation is much less clear. It's harder to get alignment on the factors truly underlying the problem and the time frame is longer, making it much more difficult to plan and implement a successful solution, i.e. you may not know if a solution works for one to three years.

Wicked problems

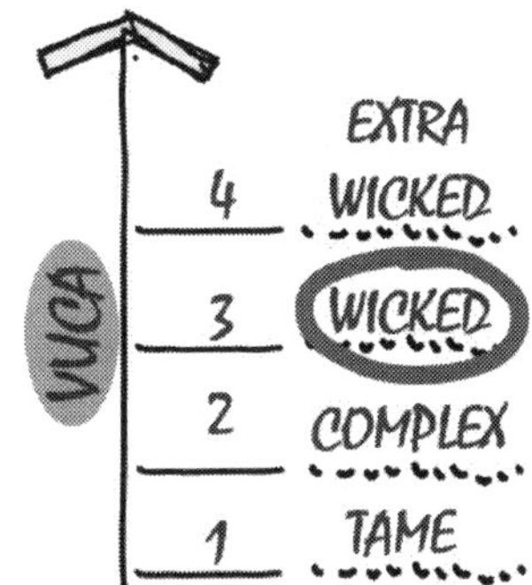

With good performance, we progress to a more senior executive level in the organization, where the problems we face and decisions we make affect the whole organization. We're now confronting Wicked problems. For anyone who's made this transition, you know it's the most difficult transition of all because of:

- High volatility – the problem is constantly changing, defying isolation as a discrete, contained problem. The changes are bigger and in some instances truly transformational, requiring significant shifts to multiple systems or processes across the whole business;

- High unfamiliarity – you're now focused on the whole organization and dealing with new external stakeholders with competing agendas to your own – even when a problem looks familiar it's actually unique, for example, it crosses new jurisdictions, regulatory regimes or cultures that distort meaning;

- High complexity – the problem intertwines with multiple systems across the whole organization or across multiple organizations.

Problems are interconnected with one another – as you solve one it transforms into another equally difficult problem, and a bad decision can have catastrophic implications for the whole organization (even the industry as a whole); and

- High ambiguity – there are multiple explanations for the problem and no way to truly test solutions as they can take many years to play out; you may not know if a solution works for three to 10 years.

Extra-Wicked problems

Extra-Wicked problems are similar to Wicked problems except the levels of volatility, unfamiliarity, complexity and ambiguity are much higher – they often represent some of the biggest, thorniest, challenges we face in the world.

Because Tame, Complex and Wicked problems are most commonly faced by most organizations, this is where we will place our focus.

Is VUCA rising for your organization?

Because rising VUCA affects the difficulty of organizational problems, executives notice significant differences in the way they and their organizations function from the way they did in the recent past.

Symptoms are everywhere. For instance, executives notice external threats are more numerous and moving faster – more of them are Wicked.

In a recent survey of 1500 CEOs, 50% felt their companies couldn't effectively deal with levels of problem difficulty they currently face and 80% were convinced those levels were rising.

These Wicked problems often demand organization-wide solutions, requiring changes that are widespread and big (transformational), pushing everyone into new and uncomfortably risky situations they've never seen before. It gets tougher to land on the right strategic solution, and even great ones generate dozens of new Complex problems and hundreds (sometimes thousands) of Tame ones.

As a result, many organizations are now in a state of perpetual change, with most organizational strategies, processes, and systems under relentless attack. These changes shift roles and capabilities within organizations and create a host of talent and performance problems as formerly capable people struggle to adapt.

As VUCA rises, the need for strategic time does as well. Executives can't hope to effectively tackle increasingly difficult problems if they can't get out of the weeds.

Conclusion

The evidence suggests that there's a big problem – VUCA is rising, making disruption much more common and severe. Uber is a classic example of a disruptor completely upsetting thousands of incumbents virtually overnight, and it's not the only example, as Amazon, Airbnb, Expedia, and Netflix have similarly disrupted thousands of incumbents in their own industries and beyond.

Executives leading incumbent organizations are particularly vulnerable to disruption, facing problems of unprecedented difficulty that affect their whole organizations. The strategic time needed to address these concerns has never been more important.

Topics we covered in Chapter 1 – Is there a problem?

Topic	Page
• Evidence suggests that there's a big problem	1
• What's causing the increase in organizational struggle and failure?	2
• VUCA is the underlying problem	3
• Is our organizational environment becoming more disruptive?	4
• Are organizations prepared for rising VUCA?	6
• Digging deeper into problem difficulty	8
• Tame problems	9
• Complex problems	10
• Wicked problems	11
• Extra-Wicked problems	12
• Is VUCA rising for your organization?	12
• Conclusion	13

2 WHO IS RESPONSIBLE FOR PREVENTING ORGANIZATIONAL STRUGGLE AND FAILURE?

'The buck stops here.' – Harry S. Truman

Some executives are in denial

YEARS AGO, I was working with the senior executive team of a large organization, and a discussion ensued about why the team was unable to maintain consistent strategic focus. I grabbed a flipchart to record their reasons and in 20 minutes filled 13 full flipchart pages. Not one reason placed any responsibility on the team. Finally, a team member said (with chagrin), 'Folks, these are excuses. Looking at all of this, I'd say we're the problem.' It was only then that they started getting to the real reasons they were so stuck in the weeds.

The primary role of executives – solving highest-level problems

While everyone in an organization is impacted by VUCA, executives are most responsible for its effect on the organization.

As a result, when organizations struggle or fail to adapt to their external environment, it's due to senior executive failure. On the surface that may sound harsh, but let's explore the executive role to understand why it's true.

An organization's CEO has a fiduciary responsibility (a legal and/or ethical relationship of trust) to his/her board for the overall success of the organization. Essentially, their primary role is to achieve one overarching objective – make the strategic choices necessary to increase shareholder value. (Although this objective has been recently challenged by some CEOs to include an equally strong focus on key stakeholder value).[(1)]

To meet this objective, CEOs must ensure they solve the problems that represent the biggest threats to shareholder value – what I call the organization's highest-level problems (HLP). For instance, if an organization is threatened by Wicked problems, that's where the CEO must focus because these problems represent much bigger threats than Complex or Tame ones. Essentially, organizational strategies are solutions to highest-level problems.

However, highest-level problems are often so difficult that a CEO typically can't solve them on their own, so they assemble a group of senior executives they feel are most capable of supporting them – the senior executive team.

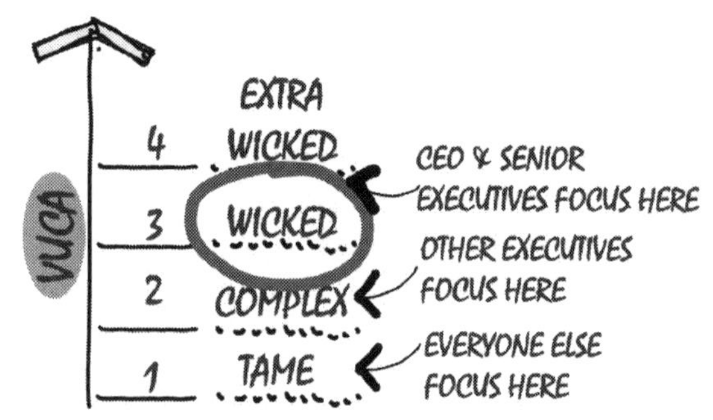

I like Peter Drucker's assertion that an executive is anyone 'who by virtue of their position or knowledge is responsible for a contribution that materially affects the capacity of the organization to perform and obtain results.' [2] However, it's imperative that executives focus on where their position or knowledge makes the greatest contribution. For senior executives, it's highest-level problems, and for all other executives, it's lower-level problems.

A deeper dive into the role of senior executives

The senior executive team is a group almost as heavily invested as the CEO is in creating strategies that effectively solve highest-level problems.

As a result, despite all that's been written on the role of executives, they essentially have just two areas of primary responsibility: strategy formulation and oversight of strategy execution (often referred to as operational oversight).

Strategy development includes responsibilities like analyzing and working through issues presented by the external environment, contributing to long-term direction-setting and strategy formulation, ensuring the organization's operating model is designed to deliver on the strategy, establishing internal and external networks to gather and transmit information, mobilizing the organization in support of the strategy, etc.

The oversight of strategy execution includes responsibilities like developing long-range strategies for their department or function that align to the organizational strategy, ensuring roles are filled with the leadership/talent demanded by the strategy, creating a strategy-supporting culture through appropriate policies, procedures, processes etc., building internal relationships that facilitate cross-departmental effectiveness, adjusting strategy based on operational feedback, etc.

Everything an executive does should be in service of strategy development and the oversight of execution. Both are equally critical – executives hoping to exchange one for the other are shirking a key responsibility – executives are always responsible for working on the business (strategy development) and working in the business (strategy execution).

Executives are stuck in the weeds

We have already seen that problems come in four sizes or levels of difficulty, and every reasonably sized organization is likely to face problems in the first three levels regularly.

For a senior executive in an organization facing Wicked problems, 'the weeds' are Complex and Tame problems – problems lower in difficulty than the ones the organization needs them to focus on.

Weeds have always been a natural part of the executive experience because of two basic realities of organizational life. First, as people rise in seniority, the number of people expecting access to them increases exponentially. At the start of a career, your immediate boss, coworkers and a few clients or customers might have a hold over you. As a senior team member, your colleagues, the board, many employees, key stakeholders and clients, regulators, consultants, industry groups, etc. expect access to you, and they're constantly accosting you with their problems.

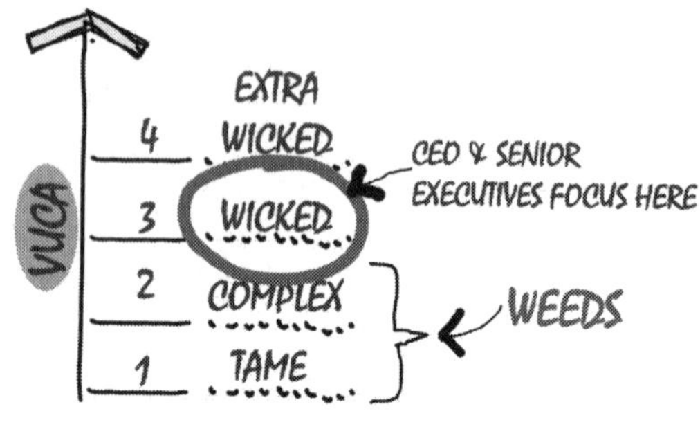

Second, in high-VUCA environments, the weeds multiply exponentially because every solution to a Wicked problem generates loads of Complex and Tame problems as changes in strategy inevitably mean changes to systems, policies, processes, roles, relationships, etc. – these changes pull executives down into the weeds as their people struggle with the challenges of strategic execution.

While it's impossible for any executive to avoid the weeds entirely, as VUCA rises, it's imperative that they carefully manage the time they spend there or risk losing focus on their primary responsibilities – working with other senior executives to develop and execute strategies that effectively solve highest-level problems.

All of this probably sounds patently obvious – not even worth stating. However, in research with senior executives I conducted in 2019, of those surveyed:

- 75% say they spend too little time working together with other senior executives on the organization's highest-level problems;

- Less than 10% say they're personally spending as much time on highest-level problems as they should;

- 85% say the majority of time they spend with other executives is typically focused on Tame problems – problems with a timeline of less than one year; and

- 60% are not aligned on the three highest-level problems facing the organization.

These results are consistent with a number of other studies. It's clear that executives are struggling to escape the weeds and make strategic time.

It's no wonder then that in my work with senior executive teams I regularly see a significant gap between where they need to focus and where they're actually focusing – most spend the bulk of their time at least one full level of problem difficulty lower than they should.

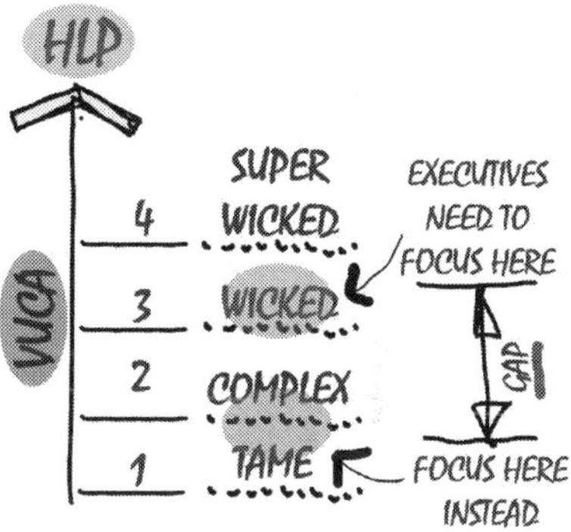

Executives must commit to getting out of the weeds for many reasons and these are the top three. First, highest-level problems demand significant time and focus from senior executives – identifying, understanding and solving them requires far more effort than lower-level problems. Second, it takes more time to rally the organization behind big strategic solutions as you gather support and manage change. Third, only senior executives have the organizational authority to develop and oversee organizational strategy. When they're stuck in the weeds, no one's working on highest-level problems.

nior executives in the weeds drive everyone into the weeds

Does this situation sound plausible? You're an executive reporting to a senior executive who's supposed to be focused on Wicked problems but spends his/her time solving Complex ones – the ones you're supposed to be solving.

What do you do? You get out of their way by working on lower-level problems – after all, you can't work on higher-level problems than the ones your boss is working on – and promptly get in the way of those paid to focus on the very problems you're now taking on. As a result, they're forced to do the same thing to others, and over time everyone's working a level of problem difficulty lower than they should – everyone's in the weeds.

The Canadian psychologist Elliott Jaques coined the term 'redundant management' to describe this phenomenon – when executives work on lower-level problems, they render those actually responsible for those problems redundant.

As a result, lower-level problems get more senior executive attention than they deserve, and no one's working at their highest level of capability. Worse, no one's developing the capabilities needed to elevate to higher levels of problem difficulty. This is a prime reason why so many executives struggle to delegate to their direct reports – those direct reports haven't developed needed capabilities because the boss has been doing their work.

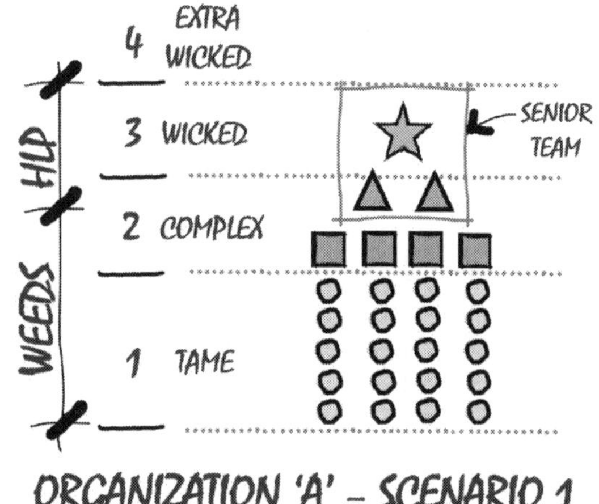

ORGANIZATION 'A' – SCENARIO 1

Let's look at four common scenarios to see the significant long-term impact this can have on an organization. In scenario 1, you see that 'Organization A' is facing highest-level (HLP) Wicked problems. The CEO (star) is focused on these problems and the VPs (triangles) are supporting them with a primary focus on highly Complex problems. The senior managers (squares) are focused on the lower-level Complex problems – managing cross-functional and departmental issues – and those reporting to them (circles) are focused on the Tame problems that typically fall within a function and department. Everyone's focused at the level of problem difficulty appropriate to their role and (presumably) level of capability.

In scenario 2, you see that 'Organization B' (a competitor) is also facing highest-level Wicked problems. However, the CEO is primarily focused on Complex problems, forcing the VPs (and everyone else) to focus on problems less difficult than the ones they should be working on. Because the senior team is in the weeds, no one is working on the Wicked problems (gap), and everyone's focused on levels of problem-difficulty that are lower than their role and level of capability.

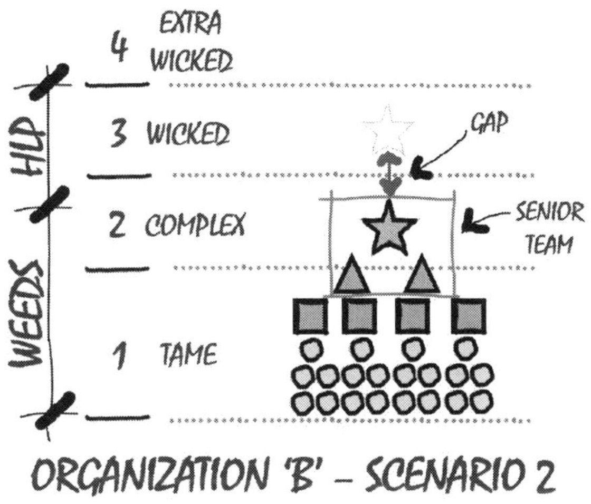

In scenario 3, for some reason the CEO of Organization B has realized that they must refocus on highest-level problems. Perhaps they're losing ground to Organization A and the CEO has realized he must elevate. Or perhaps the board has replaced the CEO with someone more willing/capable of working at higher levels of problem difficulty – a common occurrence. Now, there's a significant gap in focus and capability between where the CEO is focused and everyone else – the CEO finds themselves alone with highest-level problems because the VPs and the rest of the organization are still working at levels of problem difficulty lower n they should. The most common solution? As quickly as possible, the CEO reconstitutes the senior team – developing current VPs or recruiting new ones capable of operating at higher levels of problem difficulty.

ORGANIZATION 'B' – SCENARIO 3

In scenario 4, the CEO of Organization B has managed to reconstitute their senior team and it's more ready to tackle the organization's highest-level Wicked problems. However, there is now a significant gap between VPs and those reporting to them – VPs are consistently being pulled into the weeds, solving problems their direct reports are incapable of taking on. Typically, they'll institute a frantic effort to up-skill or recruit more capable people in key positions, but this takes time and they risk being sucked further into the weeds, with the organization returning back to scenario 2 or 3.

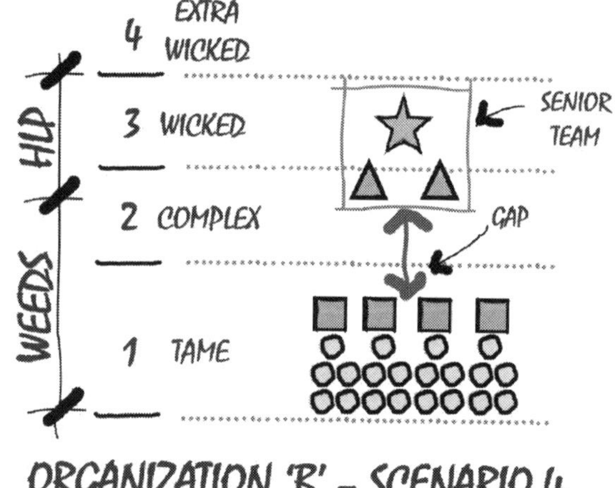

ORGANIZATION 'B' – SCENARIO 4

Most people have worked in organizations like Organization B and know that these scenarios can take years to play out. In fact, organizations often get stuck in a dangerous cycle, repeatedly moving through scenarios 2, 3 and 4, increasing the odds they'll be 'incumbents' that struggle and fail.

A senior executive – especially a CEO – dropping into the weeds forces everyone in their chain of command to drop down to a lower level of problem difficulty. It's not good for anyone.

Most executives know they're in the weeds

I've worked with many senior executives (senior executive teams) that I suspect are operating at a lower level of problem difficulty than demanded by their external environment. I ask them two questions: a) what are the sort of really big problems the organization needs to solve in order to grow and prosper; and b) what are the sort of problems you're working on?

Their answers usually demonstrate a clear recognition they're in the weeds. There's much research supporting this phenomenon. For instance, the average senior executive team spends less than three hours a month tackling strategic issues together[(3)] (some studies say it's less than one hour a month).[(11)] Only 20% of executives feel their meetings are strategic enough, [(3)] and most senior teams aren't aligned on the organizations' highest-level problems.[(4)] A 2011 McKinsey & Company report [(5)] states that just half of executives say their time spent at work aligns with their organization's strategic priorities. Finally, less than 5% of leaders say they have enough time for strategic thinking.[(6)]

Under these circumstances, it's little wonder most senior team meetings I've observed never discuss a Wicked problem unless I raise it.

Harvard Business Review reports CEOs spend 36% of their time in 'reactive mode' handling unfolding issues (routine and generally less impactful) and 70% of executives spend less than one day/ month on strategy.

There are many reasons why this is happening, and we'll touch on a number of them in Chapter 4. However, it's important to tackle one right now because it goes right to the executive's primary role and responsibilities – rising VUCA has changed the way executives must conduct strategy development and execution and many haven't adapted.

How is rising VUCA changing strategy development and execution?

Getting strategy right has always been a key executive responsibility. For instance, a survey of 1,000 corporate directors found that the number-one reason for success, and the number-one reason for failure in CEO appointments dealt with strategic alignment between the CEO and the board.(7)

Strategic development and execution are supported by the synthesis of two distinct but interrelated capabilities: strategic planning and strategic thinking. Both are critical to developing and executing effective strategies.

Strategic planning is related to overall organizational decision-making. It formalizes a system of processes and procedures that develop and communicate the strategies by which the organization will achieve success.

This has traditionally been a discrete process, and many organizations still conduct strategic planning like they always have; a planning process that culminates in a three to five-year plan outlining strategies for achieving high-level goals. Executives take responsibility for two to three strategic priorities, combine them with other operational goals or strategies, and dive into execution.

This approach to strategic planning has faced consistent criticism and resistance. For instance, over half of executives don't feel that their organization does a good job executing strategy and(8) only 5% of employees understand their organization's corporate strategy.(9)

Perhaps it's because strategic planning assumes that the challenge of setting and achieving strategic goals is primarily analytic, i.e. success will come from following a somewhat systematic, linear series of steps that often don't match up with operational or environmental realities. As a result, strategic plans are often set aside once the strategies are translated into operational plans – the image of the five-year strategic plan in mothballs is practically a meme.

Strategic thinking

According to Mintzberg and others,[10] strategic thinking 'contributes to broad, general overarching concepts that focus the future direction of an organization based on anticipated environmental concerns.'

Essentially, strategic thinking is the series of cognitive processes or activities individuals and groups use to conduct strategic planning. Strategic thinking underpins strategic planning.

Even though we all think strategically (some more effectively than others), we usually don't think about what we do to actually make it happen. Research has shown that the following seven activities contribute to effective strategic thinking:

- Reframing – challenging the underlying beliefs and assumptions behind the current state;
- Scanning – searching the external and internal environments for relevant information;
- Abstracting – grasping the essential theme or connection between apparently disparate bits of information;
- Multivariate thinking – balancing many dynamic variables simultaneously and seeing the relationships between them;
- Envisioning – based on the information gathered during reframing and scanning, imagining different future states;
- Inducting – identifying new beliefs, assumptions, and generalizations quickly from sparse data; and
- Valuating – learning and understanding the underlying values and motivations held by stakeholders.

Anyone familiar with these activities will know they demand significant time for gathering information, analysis, reflection, etc., particularly because effective strategic thinking requires the use of all seven activities, all the time.

When executives think strategically, what do they think about?

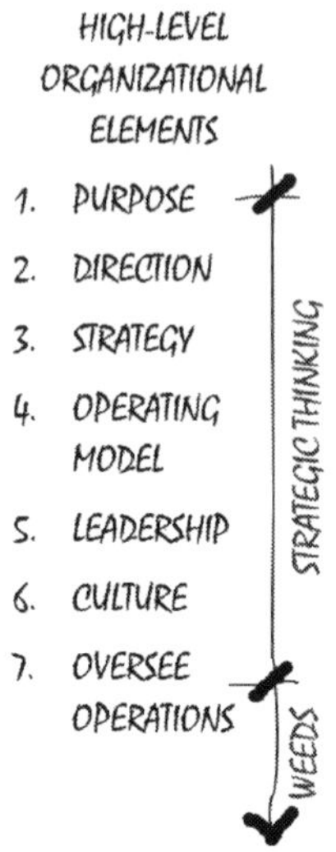

Given their organizational role, there are a series of key, high-level organizational elements that are the sole responsibility of executives – if they don't attend to them, no one does.

The first key element is establishing and maintaining organizational purpose – the reason why the organization exists. Organizations must generate revenue to survive, but most don't exist for that purpose. The revenue is used to fulfil the organization's purpose, the specific difference it is trying to make in the world.

The second key element is determining and maintaining the organization's direction – a vision, 'picture' or aspiration of what the organization will be in the future as it grows and evolves to successfully advance its purpose. This picture should be clear enough to support alignment among senior executives and can include the following pieces (among others): revenue, profit (if applicable), products/services, markets/clients, geographies, number of employees, etc. The size and complexity of the organization dictates how far into the future the picture is formed – for many organizations five years is fine, and for larger, more complex organizations it may be 10 years or more.

The third key element is determining the strategy that will best realize the organizational direction – essentially the high-level plan of action that enables the organization to navigate successfully within its environment and win against competitors, and other constraints or disruptions. The strategy is what directs the organization's resources so they take it from its current state to its desired, future state.

The fourth key element is outlining the organization's operating model – determining how the organization must structure/organize itself to most effectively deliver the strategy. The operating model delineates how roles, assets, technologies, etc. will be ordered.

The fifth key element is leadership/talent – acquiring the skillsets (through acquisition, development, etc.) that will fill the key roles (executive, technical/functional, etc.) outlined in the operating model.

The sixth key element is culture – determining the desired behaviors that will best support the strategy, designing policies, procedures, practices and processes that will drive those behaviors and managing to ensure they do.

The seventh key element is overseeing operations – ensuring the organization is delivering in alignment with the previous six elements.

When executives think strategically, they're: a) ensuring the top six elements are current, effective and in alignment, i.e. the purpose is clear, the direction supports the purpose, the strategy supports the direction, the operating model supports the strategy, and the leadership and culture required to make it all work are in place; b) effectively communicating the top six elements and overseeing management to ensure they're being effectively translated into operations on the ground; and c) monitoring how well all elements are working given the current and emerging environment, gauging how well they'll work in the future, and continuously making appropriate adjustments.

Executives find themselves in the weeds when they're diving too deeply beyond the seventh element in response to change and disruption – continuously intervening in behavioral issues and/or the implementation of policies, procedures, practices and processes within or between departments, etc. when more lasting and effective solutions are often found by rethinking the top six elements.

How does rising VUCA impact strategic planning and thinking?

As organizations face greater disruption and change, strategic thinking – and the time required to conduct it effectively – becomes an ongoing priority, resulting in more constant external and internal monitoring and redesign to allow for adjustments as conditions shift. Instead of discrete, annual, or semi-annual attention to the six elements discussed above, strategic planning and thinking become a 24/7 practice.

In high-VUCA environments, strategic plans that aren't regularly refreshed quickly lose their meaning, and the organization risks losing direction as unplanned reactions to environmental changes pull it off course. While a dedicated strategic planning process may still provide initial strategic direction and intent, the plan must be updated regularly, ideally quarterly (or more often depending on the level of disruption) to ensure new strategic thinking is translated into executable plans as soon as possible and monitored on an ongoing basis.

The agenda and cadence of strategic and operational meetings must adapt so that strategic thinking is consistently informed by new external and internal developments and operations – the link between strategy and 'events on the ground' is closer. While they oversee strategic execution, executives are constantly challenging, testing, and adapting the strategy as it's executed - using operational feedback to guide strategic choices.

All of this demands considerably more time and attention than it typically receives from most executives.

24/7 strategic thinking and the impact on executives

This demand for continuous strategic thinking has significant implications for executives. For instance, they must spend more time monitoring and understanding their external environment. They must bring more strategic thinking to all parts of their role; building long-term strategic relationships with external stakeholders and across their organizations, considering the strategic impact decisions applied to their own department and function may have on the whole organization, taking a longer-term strategic view to the development of talent, etc.

Executives operating in high-VUCA environments must exercise greater 'managerial discretion' – the ability to deal with external and internal issues as quickly and forcefully as possible, even when actions are in conflict with board/ownership's thinking. They also need to negotiate that discretion with their boards.

Because rising VUCA increases problem difficulty, highest-level problems become too tough for individuals to tackle on their own, so executive groups or teams must build the capability needed to solve them collectively – a time-consuming process in itself.

Finally, VUCA puts pressure on an executive's individual strategic-thinking capability. We all know people who seem to be naturally strategic, with an uncanny ability to quickly cut through complexity and see the big picture. For the rest of us, the development of strategic thinking capability takes experience – learning and regularly applying (practicing) the seven strategic thinking activities to real-life strategic issues.

Even with solid strategic-thinking capability, coping in high-VUCA environments is challenging. For instance, imagine you're an executive in a traditional taxi company when another traditional competitor moves into your market. This is a Complex problem involving some significant changes to how you operate, but you've seen something like this before; you understand their business because it's like your own, know how to differentiate yourself, and have the relationships with the key stakeholders, regulators, etc. that you'll need to protect yourself.

Now, pretend you're that same executive when Uber first hits town. This is now a Wicked problem. No one you know has seen anything like this. Uber is completely unlike you – they don't own a single cab – you know nothing about how they'll differentiate themselves, and when you do learn (from quick, bitter experience) you're completely unprepared to compete. Your previous knowledge and relationships don't help nearly as much. In this new environment, the ability to think strategically is the only hope you have.

For executives, 24/7 strategic thinking changes almost everything about their role and they can't do it effectively if they can't get out of the weeds.

The personal impact of mishandled VUCA

Many executives can describe the toll that rising VUCA has on their life and career because most are scrambling to keep pace. They're in a constant state of overwhelm and feel like things are beyond their control. Under those circumstances, it's little wonder that 50-60% of executives fail within the first 18 months of a new role, and over half feel they're being held accountable for problems beyond their control.[11]

When senior executives start to struggle and fail, the board/ownership often starts questioning whether the CEO and their team can effectively take the organization forward. The mistrust and misalignment that's created is draining for all concerned.

If things don't turn around, the board recruits a new CEO – as VUCA rises, so does the CEO attrition rate, now nearly 15% per year in North America.[12] But executive change doesn't stop there, as a new CEO typically replaces 70% of the existing senior team within two years.[13]

This senior level disruption cascades through the executive ranks[13] and affects most employees in the organization – in fact there's solid evidence to suggest that excessive senior executive transition is bad for organizations[14] – but it is hardest for those new executives under pressure to reverse fortunes quickly. Typically, they encounter a wary board, a flurry of turnaround strategies and initiatives to execute with a workforce lacking the desire and capabilities needed to pull it off. This all forces them into the weeds as they abandon the strategic high ground and start reacting to problems in the field.

It's no wonder that within two years, 25-45% of these new executives are considered to be 'failing', and most rate significant work transitions like these as more difficult life events than divorce or the loss of a direct family member.[13]

Clearly, the inability of executives to counter rising VUCA effectively is having a significant organizational and personal toll. In fact, an inability to get out of the weeds is a significant career threat.

Conclusion

Without question, executives are responsible for the success and struggle or failure of their organizations. Full stop.

They carry out these responsibilities in two primary ways: by developing strategy and overseeing its execution. Despite this clarity, many executives are (knowingly) stuck in the weeds, spending too much time on lower-level problems at the expense of the highest-level problems they're paid to solve.

This creates a host of issues. For instance, executives fail to build an effective strategic planning process and/or the personal and collective strategic thinking capability needed to cope with rising VUCA and disruption. They inadvertently stunt the development of those they lead by driving everyone into the weeds and put their own careers at risk as boards react to strategic ineffectiveness.

I believe when executives can't get out of the weeds, the organizations they lead are at greater risk of struggle and failure.

Topics we covered in Chapter 2 – Who is responsible for preventing organizational struggle and failure?

Topic	Page
• Some executives are in denial	15
• The primary role of executives – solving highest-level problems	16
• A deeper dive into the role of senior executives	17
• Executives are stuck in the weeds	17
• Senior executives in the weeds drive everyone into the weeds	20
• Most executives know they're in the weeds	23
• How is rising VUCA changing strategy development and execution?	24
• Strategic thinking	25
• When executives think strategically, what do they think about?	26
• How does rising VUCA impact strategic planning and thinking	27
• 24/7 strategic thinking and the impact on executives	28
• The personal impact of mishandled VUCA	29
• Conclusion	30

3 WHY DO EXECUTIVES STRUGGLE AND FAIL?

'Success is not final, failure is not fatal: it is the courage to continue that counts.' –*Winston Churchill*

Some executive teams don't function very strategically

AS PART OF my work with senior executive teams, I like to watch the team in action. I stand back, observe, and assess as they undertake strategic dialogue like they might do if I wasn't present.

Once, I watched as a team was working its way through a difficult discussion on the organization's future direction. The team leader wasn't happy about where things were heading, so he sat at the back of the room, head down, with his back to the rest of the group, without uttering a single word for the full two-hour discussion.

Another team was undertaking a similar exercise with a long serving, strong-willed CEO looking to push more responsibility to his senior team. After they presented a bold new vision and strategy, he stood and (angrily) declared, 'It's obvious from this no one's happy with the leadership I've provided all these years. I'm not one to stay where I'm not wanted.' With that, he left the room and refused to attend further meetings.

Another team met for a two-hour strategic dialogue. No one could remember the strategic initiatives they were responsible for leading. The first 90 minutes were consumed with operational presentations from direct reports, and the final 30 minutes were spent designing a PowerPoint summary of those presentations for their board.

These situations aren't indicative of most senior teams. I'm certain your senior team is working much, much more effectively. However, for most, a significant gap exists between current performance and what's needed to effectively tackle highest-level problems.

The need to improve executive effectiveness

Due to rising VUCA, executives now face more disruption. More organizations are struggling and failing to adapt, and the number of CEOs responsible for building strategies intended to counter disruption are increasingly losing their jobs, with members of their senior team often following suit. Clearly, executives are struggling to adapt to the new challenges presented by rising VUCA.

So, why is this happening? Executives are generally smart, hardworking and ambitious; shouldn't they be able to adapt? The answer is yes, of course. Most will adapt.

However, doing so requires a firm commitment to improving executive effectiveness and as we will see, this can't be done without making strategic time.

How do we build executive effectiveness?

We build executive effectiveness the same way we build any capability – we learn it.

As infants, we start life not knowing how to do very much and proceed through a process of learning that enables some to become executives leading complicated, sophisticated organizations in high-VUCA environments.

Martin Broadwell first advanced the four stages of learning model (also called the Conscious Competence Model) in 1969, suggesting that all learning starts with not knowing something and advances through four stages that increase 'consciousness' and 'competence'. Consciousness is the recognition that we must improve our skill in an area and acquiring the knowledge necessary to do so. Competence is using that knowledge to apply the skill effectively.

If you doubt that, think about an activity you've become really good at, and notice that most or all of the deficiencies you had when you started have been overcome as you progressed through the Conscious Competence Model.

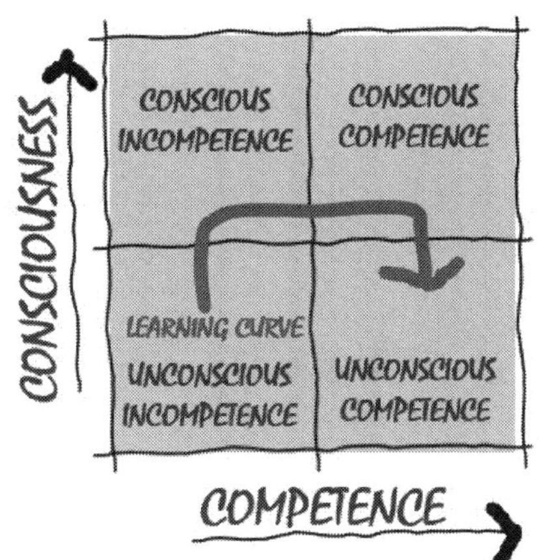

Think of your shoelaces for example. We start life not knowing we even need to tie shoelaces (unconscious incompetence). We're told that we need to learn how to tie them and start practicing, making lots of mistakes along the way (conscious incompetence). As we practice, we get further advice, until we tie them well, as long as we think about it (conscious competence). Finally, we tie them well without thinking about it at all (unconscious competence).

Getting better at anything is simply the desire to improve, combined with a good learning experience. Of course, this won't mean all executives are equally capable because some have much better learning experiences; they apply themselves more, have better teachers, etc. or have a natural head start (superior cognitive abilities or specific personality traits). When they combine this natural head start with great learning experiences, they have the potential to be better at some things than most other people.

However, executives with desire and access to great learning experiences can significantly develop any capability – including strategic thinking capability, regardless of any natural head start.

Unless of course they can't make the time needed to gain the knowledge and practice.

What attributes do executives need to learn and develop?

There are many models that explain how executives build greater effectiveness.

Based on research and my own experience working with hundreds of executives, I believe four highly interrelated attributes are key to building effectiveness. They include the ability to: a) create executive impact; b) exercise executive role effectiveness; c) make sound individual and collective decisions; and d) make and maintain strategic time and focus.

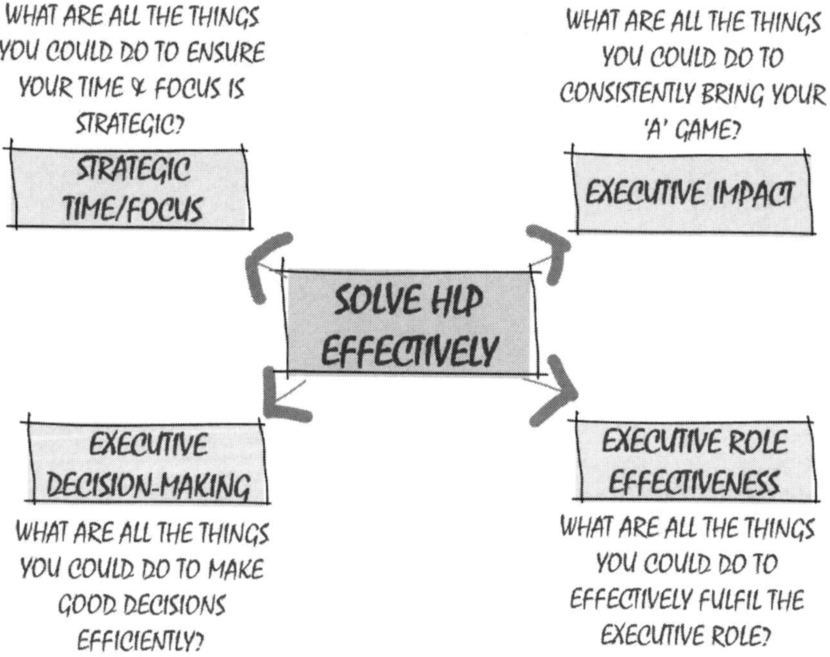

Executive impact

The role of executives in a modern organization is very challenging. They lead their department or function and are recognized as a leader across much of the organization. They're always on, interacting with a broad cross section of people, over long hours, in high-pressure situations over time.

The ability to have executive impact is important for inspiring, motivating, and energizing others to provide discretionary effort and elevate their performance. It's a key executive tool because the leader can account for 70% of the difference between engaged and disengaged employees.[1] Evidence suggests there's room for improvement as employee engagement is dangerously low in most organizations, with almost 70% of employees not engaged or actively disengaged[2]. Executive impact is supported by a desire to take on big strategic problems, the will and passion to seek challenging leadership roles, personality and motivational preferences that drive inspiring leadership behavior, and the ability to maximize areas of personal strength.

Deficiencies in these characteristics can reduce executive impact. For instance, personality and motivational preferences for stability, deliberation and risk reduction can significantly limit an executive's impact under conditions that demand bold change, decisiveness, and risk-taking.[3]

Executive role effectiveness

As we've seen, the principal role of an executive is to support the CEO in developing and executing strategies that increase shareholder value. However, rising VUCA has changed the nature of this role and many have not kept pace.

The ability to adapt to this new strategic reality demands a capacity for driving innovation and change, taking a long-term, strategic view, navigating and impacting the external environment effectively, and providing high-level technical or functional solutions that advance the organization.

Deficiencies in these characteristics can reduce role effectiveness. For instance, an inability to carry out the seven activities necessary for effective strategic thinking (reviewed in Chapter 2) might encourage executives to drop into the weeds, where problems are more familiar and success is more assured.

Executive decision-making

It isn't enough to solve difficult problems; solutions must be effectively translated into decisions that hundreds (and sometimes thousands) of others can successfully implement. Bad decisions can have very negative organizational consequences.

The ability to make sound business decisions as consistently as possible demands a capability for successfully solving Complex and Wicked problems, exercising good business/commercial judgment, utilizing the strength of groups and teams to make good decisions collectively, and getting others to align.

Deficiencies in these characteristics can reduce role effectiveness. For instance, a 2006 study indicated that groups of three to five people perform better on complex problem solving than the best of an equivalent number of individuals.[4] Yet my own strategic time survey showed 75% of executives feel their senior team spends less time than necessary on highest-level problems, and most are not aligned on the biggest problems demanding their focus.

STRATEGIC TIME
& FOCUS
+
EXECUTIVE IMPACT
+
EXECUTIVE ROLE
EFFECTIVENESS
+
EXECUTIVE
DECISION-MAKING

SOLVE HLP

Make strategic time – stay out of the weeds

Take your strongest group of executives. People with strong executive impact, the capabilities needed to carry out their executive role effectively, and who consistently make sound strategic and operational decisions. Task them with making and implementing a critical high-level decision, then drive them into the weeds with irrelevant distractions, less critical and unrelated issues (or watch them do this to themselves), add an overwhelming schedule, and see how well they perform.

It's easy to see how executives get pulled into the weeds. They don't prioritize their time, push back on issues below their pay grade, or even know where their time goes. They can't unblock their calendars and are their own worst enemy, making decisions that pull them, and those they lead, into the weeds.

Strategic time is the most personally and organizationally valuable time an executive can undertake. It's when our biggest challenges are explored and considered and where life and organizationally altering decisions are made – the sort of big decisions that affect the thousands of smaller decisions that flow from them. When we're in the weeds and can't/won't make strategic time, we're executives in name and title only because we aren't performing an executive's true role.

The inability to make strategic time is a tragic organizational waste of an executive's capability and talent, negatively impacting those they lead and their own career.

The fundamental reason for ineffective executives – lack of strategic time

I believe the fundamental reason for organizational struggle and failure is lack of executive strategic time and focus. I take this view because no matter how smart, capable and motivated you are, if you don't make time for something, nothing's going to happen.

No strategic time means no strategic thinking, no time to inspire and elevate the effort of others, no time to execute the executive role effectively, and no time to confront disruption and solve highest-level problems. Simply put, for executives, making strategic time is table stakes.

There are other compelling reasons why getting out of the weeds and making strategic time is so critical.

Time is the basis of production

To produce anything, we have to consider time. Everything we do in organizational life has a deadline – we commit to doing everything 'by some point in time.'

The first consideration in determining the production of anything, be it baking cakes, making decisions, building relationships, developing strategy, etc., is related to the 'limiting step' (5) – the step in the process that limits all other steps because it's the slowest or the hardest to complete.

Executives put considerable effort into managing capital, real estate, people, etc., yet time – the only finite resource and the one that underpins the effectiveness of all other resources – is relatively unmanaged. Executives tacitly assume they (and others) will 'find time' when it hasn't been properly allocated.

Executives exist to develop and execute strategy, and strategic time is a critical limiting step.

Time management is a barometer for 'executive function'

In psychology, the term 'executive function' refers to the brain's ability to carry out five sophisticated functions impacting problem-solving capability: paying attention, organizing and planning, initiating tasks (and staying focused on them), regulating emotions, and self-monitoring.

These functions are critical to learning and problem-solving, and without knowing it, executives use them constantly.

However, struggles to make strategic time may indicate deficiencies in other areas of executive effectiveness. For instance, does it indicate a lack of discipline in all areas of work when you struggle to place attention on the most timely priorities? Does a permanently blocked calendar indicate an inability to maintain focus on a manageable set of tasks? Do frustration and a sense of being overwhelmed indicate some emotional immaturity that affects other parts of your career and life? Does your inability to take firm control of your calendar indicate a lack of self-control that impedes other endeavors?

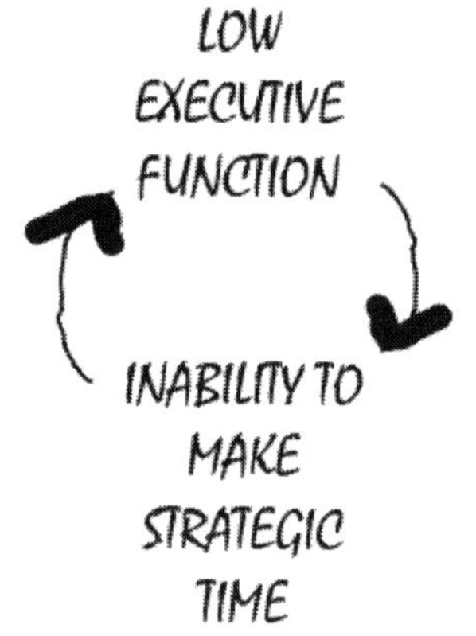

Making strategic time is a litmus test and an opportunity to develop and apply executive functions that strengthen all aspects of your work and life.

Time is fundamental to learning

Becoming an executive is typically a big step into a completely new level of problem difficulty, and the capabilities that 'got you here won't get you there' – you must develop or die.

Unlike athletes or actors, executives can't spend 99% of their time practicing for a two to three-hour performance. They're always 'on', learning 'on-the-job' and/or 'off the side of their desk'. As a result, their learning is mostly experience based – no experience, no learning.

Learning through experience is daunting because you have to meet performance expectations, i.e. deliver efficiently with high quality while you learn, and it takes dedicated effort over time.

If you want to get a quick sense for how much dedicated effort and time it takes, try the following experiment. Take a piece of paper and write your signature on it. Then just below that, write it again with your other hand, and notice the difference between the two.

Most notice that the second signature takes a lot longer to write, i.e. it's uncomfortable, you have to think about what you're doing (low efficiency), and the quality is much lower (low quality) – that's what conscious incompetence feels like.

Compare this time and effort to that required for solving very difficult, high-level problems and it's clear that without making the significant strategic time needed to build strategic-thinking capability, you'll always be consciously incompetent.

Time is fundamental to highest-level problem solving

Naturally, Tame problems take much less time to solve than Wicked ones. Quick individual effort or consultation usually addresses the former, while the latter might be virtually unsolvable.

Simply defining Wicked problems demands a lot of time – as Albert Einstein put it, 'If I had an hour to solve a problem, I'd spend 55 minutes thinking about the problem and five minutes thinking about solutions.' Studies show that trying to solve very Complex/Wicked problems without time for adequate analysis can lead to over-simplification and failure.[(6)]

Complex and Wicked problems demand time for monitoring the environment inside and outside the organization, much of it hard to discern. Gathering information from stakeholders often means developing new relationships – a time-consuming process in its own right. Most high-level problems are best tackled by teams, another significant drag on time. Because complexity and ambiguity is high, understanding the problem takes time, and because wicked problems generate lots of potential courses of action, additional time for individual and collective reflection, design, decision-making (often collaborative), alignment and follow-up is needed.

Clearly, effectively developing and executing strategy, particularly in a high-VUCA environment, is virtually impossible without strategic time.

Lack of time reduces job and life satisfaction

Studies indicate people who feel they use their time wisely have higher satisfaction in their work and lives, less stress, reduced anxiety, and more control over their lives.[7]

In the dozens of interviews I've conducted with executives snared in the weeds, they regularly reflect frustration and a sense of overwhelm that negatively impacts all facets of their work and life. They feel guilty because they can't focus on those aspects of their role they know are critical; they can't solve problems as effectively as they could with more time, and the constant juggle of work with personal time is a constant source of anxiety and concern.

Many feel that they're out of control and failing. Unfortunately, without making strategic time, they might be right.

Conclusion

There are a number of reasons why executives fail to prevent organizational struggle and failure, and it's seldom because they're not working hard enough. It may be that they lack the leadership, technical or functional capability needed to lead at their level in the organization or haven't learned how to effectively carry out their role as an executive. It may be a lack of individual and collective capability for making highest-level decisions, particularly in highly disruptive environments. However, even when these elements are firmly in place, executives are bound to struggle and fail if they can't make strategic time. When it comes to effectively meeting the executive's role and responsibilities, making strategic time is table stakes.

Topics we covered in Chapter 3 – Why do executives struggle and fail?

Topic	Page
• Some executive teams don't function very strategically	33
• The need to improve executive effectiveness	34
• How do we build executive effectiveness?	34
• What attributes do executives need to learn and develop?	36
• Executive impact	36
• Executive role effectiveness	37
• Executive decision-making	37
• Make strategic time - stay out of the weeds	38
• The fundamental reason for ineffective executives – lack of strategic time	39
• Time is the basis of production	39
• Time management is a barometer for 'executive function'	40
• Time is fundamental to learning	40
• Time is fundamental to highest-level problem solving	41
• Lack of time reduces job and life satisfaction	42
• Conclusion	42

WHAT PREVENTS EXECUTIVES FROM MAKING AND MAINTAINING STRATEGIC TIME?

'Executives are working as hard as they ever did. It is difficult to see how they could work harder. For the corporation man, the balanced life is as elusive as ever, possibly more so.' – William H. Whyte Jr. from his study of 'management men' in 1954.

It's not for a lack of time or effort

BEFORE WE DIVE into the reasons why executives struggle to escape the weeds, let's look at where their time currently goes and hopefully uncover opportunities for big improvements.

Interestingly, getting an accurate view of executive time is challenging, as most executives keep poor time records and inaccurately report their time, often overinflating time at work by eight to 12 hours a week.(1) Furthermore, different time-measurement methodologies yield different results. The way the information is reported can make it difficult to apply to your situation, and executive roles can vary so much that one person's ideal schedule might not work for anyone else.

To control for different methodologies/reporting techniques, we'll pick one study, conducted by Michael Porter and Nitin Nohria and presented in a 2018 Harvard Business Review article 'The Leader's Calendar,'[(2)] as our standard (although other methodologies have produced different results). This study focuses on CEOs, so can't be directly extrapolated to every executive's situation, but it does provide useful guidance.

Everyone agrees we all get 168 hours per week (no one gets more or less time, no matter how capable they are), and an executive is awake for 119 of those on average (assuming an average of seven hours sleep a night).

While awake, they spend 62.5 hours working – 53% of their waking time. This might seem very high, as it works out to 12.5 hours per day when spread over a five-day work week, but it includes time on weekends and vacations (executives spend some time working on 79% of weekend days and 70% of vacation days) so that time's spread out over a full seven-day work week. As a result, over a full year, the average North American executive spends a whopping 3,250 hours on the job.

On average, North American CEOs work 62.5 hours/week, every week of the year (this amount includes the time spent on weekends and vacations). This equates to 3,250 hours/year - almost double the time of a salaried employee.

That's a lot, especially contrasted with the average worker who spends about 1800 hours on the job (based on a 37.5-hour work week and four weeks of vacation, statutory holidays, etc.) – a 1,450 hour difference; about 39 additional weeks of work per year.

While North American executives work harder than those in most other countries, they can't touch Chinese executives or workers who regularly clock 72 hours per week (9:00 to 9:00 six days a week), a schedule seldom matched outside Silicon Valley.

Clearly, lack of effort and a willingness to work long hours isn't preventing executives from making strategic time. Let's see whether the four areas executives spend most of their time yields insights.

Meetings

Executives spend time in meetings far more than they spend time alone – approximately a 70/30 split. A typical executive spends about 65% of their workweek (about 40 hours) in meetings.

Meetings are a blessing – where groups create collective intelligence and establish many behavioral and cultural norms. They're also a principal method for mobilizing others – they're where most 'leadership' happens and most highest-level problems are solved.

Meetings are a curse – they waste loads of time by some combination of starting late, running longer than necessary, poor meeting management, lack of clear purpose, minimal preparation, and too many meeting participants. That's a long list of issues, and it's not close to complete.

Studies consistently show that most meetings are big time wasters (of course, you know this from experience) and represent one of the biggest opportunities for making strategic time, as we'll see in Chapter 8.

Interaction with others

An executive position makes you available to the whole organization, so it's little wonder that over 60% of an executive's time is spent interacting with others.(2)

Many of these interactions occur in meetings, but also include other forms of communication, like face-to-face interaction outside of a formal meeting, email, telephone conversations, etc. Interaction through email alone is becoming ubiquitous. For instance, while the average office worker receives 120 emails a day and sends out 40, the typical executive receives more than 200 emails per workday and sends over 70 per workday to others.(3) For some CEOs, email can consume almost a quarter of their day.(4)

Dealing with information

Because strategic thinking is an executive's stock-in-trade, they consume loads of information in the form of reports, journals, news sources, and books, much more extensively than the average person does.

For instance, many executives read up to 50–60[5] books per year and spend considerable time at conferences and/or accessing information through other sources. None of this includes time spent on social media, which is climbing rapidly – podcasts, Facebook, Tumblr, Instagram, Twitter, Snapchat and LinkedIn being some of the prime culprits.

The amount of time the average executive spends reading and reflecting on information ranges from one to one-and-a-half hours a day or seven to 11 hours a week.

Performance management and people development

Executives direct and oversee those responsible for executing organizational strategies, and a key responsibility is ensuring that those they direct are capable now and in the future.

This requires time dedicated in two distinct but closely related areas; performance management and talent development.

Performance management is ensuring that those currently working in the organization are consistently meeting and elevating performance standards. Talent development is ensuring the organization will have the skills and capabilities needed in the future.

Time spent in these two areas varies widely. Executives dedicated to both might spend three to four weeks[6] over the course of a year (about 6–8% of their time) setting development strategies/plans, overseeing execution and development, providing coaching, mentoring, sponsoring, and other opportunities for building talent and evaluating performance over time.

Others spend much less time on this, however, they'll likely spend up to double that amount of time[7] in conflict resolution, remedial development, or a related activity resulting from poor performance. As a result, whether the experience is proactive or reactive, executives will spend somewhere between 10-15% of their time in talent/performance management.

What the data tells me

When I look at the data presented above, I don't see how executives can make strategic time by working longer hours – most are already pushing the limits of endurance over the long term. While significantly limiting meetings and interactions with others and/or drastically reducing information, performance, and talent management will create time, it's just as important to refocus as much of this activity as possible on highest-level problems instead of more weeds. For instance, 65% of time spent in meetings might be OK if the majority of that time is spent on highest-level problems.

Of course, executives know this. They know the number of organizations struggling and failing is increasing, and that elevated VUCA is increasing problem difficulty. They also know it's their job to develop and oversee the strategies needed to meet this challenge, and it all won't work without making strategic time.

They know all this then admit they're not making the strategic time needed to get the job done. Why is this happening?

It's not all about time-saving tools and techniques

I'm convinced that time-saving tools and techniques are part of the answer, but not the full story because if that's all it took, a majority of executives wouldn't say getting out of the weeds is one of their primary challenges.[(8)]

I believe the psychological and social barriers to making strategic time thwart most executives. For instance, in the strategic time survey I recently conducted, half of the respondents indicated that their efforts to make strategic time were hindered by 'personal reluctance'.

As a coach, I believe many barriers are the result of unintended consequences or behaviors that made perfect sense before you became an executive but don't any longer, and/or serve you well in one part of your life but create problems elsewhere.

Unintended consequences are outcomes of a purposeful action that are not intended or foreseen, and they're pervasive. Here's just one example of how unconscious personality preferences can drive us into the weeds.

Conscientiousness is a personality trait that measures the degree to which people are businesslike, persistent, thorough, and dependable.

Highly conscientious people tend to seek out challenges to prove their capability, are unfailingly reliable in most situations, can drive themselves through challenging or unpleasant tasks, and push themselves very hard to achieve success.

I bet that describes you, because personality assessments consistently show executives score highly for conscientiousness compared to the general population.[9] Conscientiousness isn't a tool or technique, it's part of our identity – how we see ourselves and how we want others to see us – so we unconsciously apply it to every facet of our life. In other words, when we're highly conscientious, we tend to do it to a fault.

For example, I asked a successful, highly conscientious executive about his work. He said, 'I love it, it's the most important thing in my life. I'd work 12 hours a day, seven days a week if I could.'

I asked if this ever creates problems. He said, 'It used to, but my wife convinced me I needed to relax more so I started playing golf and it's going great. In fact, if I work really hard at it, I think I can be club champion within three years.'

Ask someone with high conscientiousness to take on any task and they'll likely see it as a challenge, an opportunity to excel and prove (to you and themselves) how persistent and dependable they are. They'll take it on even when they shouldn't – even when it's a lower-level problem – and they'll keep taking on new tasks even when they're overwhelmed.

So, before highly conscientious executives will make strategic time, they have to be satisfied that doing so won't change the way they see themselves or how they want to be perceived by others. However, once they're satisfied, you can count on them to make strategic time as conscientiously as possible.

Getting out of the weeds is a change challenge

In his book, *The Effective Executive*, Peter Drucker writes, 'The most common cause of executive failure is inability or unwillingness to change with the demands of a new position. The executive who fails to understand this will suddenly do the wrong things the wrong way, even though he does exactly what in his old job had been the right things done the right way.'

Changing behavior involves two steps. First, form a strong intention to change. An intention signals a desire to make a change in behavior, and the stronger it is, the more likely you'll succeed (no guarantees though).

Because it's so critical to behavior change, psychologists have studied the subject of intention for years, identifying three success factors that strengthen intention.*

First, the benefits gained by changing outweigh the benefits offered by the status quo, and/or the consequences suffered by not changing aren't serious enough to compel change. Second, whether you or others approve or disapprove of the new behavior. Third, whether the change is something you believe you're capable of doing.

When all these factors strongly favor change, our intention is likely durable enough to overcome barriers. When one or more doesn't favor change, intention is weakened.

The second step to effectively changing behavior is to take action ASAP, otherwise strong intentions can fade over time. Two success factors strengthen action – guidance and accountability; having someone (or a number of people) who can guide your progress with informed feedback and hold you accountable for the change.

In my coaching, executives often describe the unintended consequences of organizational policies, processes, leaders, colleagues, culture, etc. that inadvertently block their intention and efforts to make strategic time. Let's expose some common ones – not so you can use them as excuses or reasons to stay in the weeds, but so you can recognize and course correct when you find yourself headed that way.

** The factors vary depending on the theory of change you are using – these three come from the Theory of Planned Behavior initially proposed by Icek Ajzen.*

How 'I'm not worth it' pushes you into the weeds

Though many of us have stopped to reflect on the unique contributions we might make in the world or the objectives we might achieve, the demands of work and life can intervene and spoil our best-laid plans. Why do we let this happen?

Depending on our personality, some feel they must put the needs of others ahead of their own, while others sacrifice focus and impact for the freedom to chase knowledge and experiences for their own sake. Then there are those who feel an obligation to remain loyal to practices and people even when they should move on. As a result, we inadvertently diminish our hopes and aspirations.

That's too bad, because time truly is a finite resource, and if we're not careful, it gets away from us. In her book, *The Top Five Regrets of the Dying*, Australian palliative care nurse Bonnie Ware writes about the biggest regrets her patients express at the end of their lives. Almost all patients regretted 'spending so much of their life on the treadmill of work existence.'

If you're exercising, a treadmill allows you to walk or run in place, but it's hardly the metaphor people want applied to their career and life. Humans aspire to self-actualization, the fulfillment of one's talent, potential and aspirations – the kind of things we use strategic time to contemplate, strategize and action.

As the American psychologist Adam Grant says, 'Reflecting on a career, no one says "I wish I'd caved in more to other's expectations".' Making strategic time is the ultimate statement that says you're willing to fight to make the most of yourself – you're worth the resistance, re-learning, and change it demands.

How performance expectations push you into the weeds

Performance expectations are powerful tools for change because achieving them provides many benefits, such as financial compensation, promotion, recognition, etc.

Unfortunately, many incentives have unintended consequences because they reward behaviors that help us in one area, while inadvertently blocking our efforts in other areas, such as making strategic time.

Because short-term performance expectations are easier to set, measure and achieve than longer-term ones, our boss is likely to put more focus on them, so we do as well. Under those circumstances, making time to ensure your team hits a monthly sales target versus thinking strategically about long-term market changes feels right (especially when your team wants you focused there as well).

Most CEOs say strategic thinking is a key priority, only to pay real attention to performance that pushes you into the weeds. For instance, there's usually little recognition for great work on a strategic initiative, but plenty of notice if you miss last month's revenue projection by 1%. How often does strategic thinking take a back seat to six days of low-value scrambling as you prepare a response to an errant comment from a board member? How much strategic thinking could replace countless hours spent over-preparing for executive and/or board meetings because you're expected to have an immediate, informed answer to any query about your department, no matter how trivial the issue?

It's not unusual for a boss and their direct reports to have different performance expectations. I often start a coaching relationship with an executive by asking their boss, 'What are one to two things they most need to improve?' In different ways they all answer, 'They need to prepare to solve problems I face at my level.' However, they often fail to communicate these expectations clearly to their direct report and/or hold them accountable for improvement. Without agreeing on long-term expectations, the boss inevitably focuses on skills supporting short-term objectives.

Of course, the boss isn't the only one with performance expectations. 'Most of us feel entangled in a web of commitments from which it can be painful to extricate ourselves: we worry that we're letting our colleagues or employers down if we stop doing certain tasks – I want to look busy and productive – the company values team players.' [(10)] Many executives forsake strategic time out of concern for the expectations of colleagues and other stakeholders.

Not to mention the high-performance standards executives set for themselves. Many exhibit high diligence[(11)] and are willing to work very hard to very high standards. However, under pressure and stress, this need for high quality can make them controlling, inflexible, and reluctant to delegate – pushing them to hold on to lower-level problems that they should be giving to others.

While these are all legitimate issues, forsaking strategic thinking is a false choice that serves no one. Struggling to meet today's expectations is usually a sign that strategic decisions made two years ago could have been better. Without better strategic thinking today, many will be in the same boat two years from now.

Don't let performance expectations drive you into the weeds.

How 'Look, I'm urgent and busy' pushes you into the weeds

Years ago, I was a member of a few volunteer boards that, combined with my day job and a young family, made my life very fulfilling and extremely hectic. My terms on two of the boards ended simultaneously, and gaping holes suddenly appeared in my calendar. It was a wonderful opportunity to step back and reorient towards high-value goals. I hated it. Suddenly I wasn't in constant demand, and I didn't know what to do with myself. As a result, I quickly grabbed the first new board appointments I was offered – both unfulfilling – and regretted every minute until they ended.

As a highly conscientious, hard-working executive, how would you feel if you had nothing to do? Your initial reaction might be, 'God, I'd love it!' But would you really like your boss to notice you don't work very hard, or have those you lead question how little you seem to do? I didn't think so. I've met very few executives who answer yes and are still employed. Most get a charge out of being urgent and busy and perceived that way by others. In fact, it's so important to most executives that they're often duped into equating busyness and urgency with value-added effort, even when it clearly isn't.

When the old adage, 'don't just stand there, do something' is a guiding principle in your life (consciously or unconsciously), you're going to spend a lot of time in the weeds.

How low management discretion pushes you into the weeds

Earlier we talked about managerial discretion – the latitude executives have to set objectives and strategies different from those advocated by ownership (the board).

The level of VUCA in the environment and the organization's stage in the business life cycle determine the managerial discretion executives need to do their jobs effectively.

When current strategies work well and VUCA is low, owners of incumbent organizations grant relatively little discretion to management because they don't need or want them to disrupt a winning strategy. In these organizations, executives gravitate to lower-level problems because ownership reserves the sole right to tackle highest-level ones.

Over time, executive ranks may fill with people exemplifying a 'safe pair of hands' over entrepreneurialism – 'order takers' instead of 'order makers' – further reducing the organization's ability to respond boldly to disruption. In turn, these executives create principles, policies, culture, etc. that mirror their preferences and reduce discretion throughout the organization.[12]

When VUCA rises, the unintended consequences of this reveal themselves. For instance, the organization's strategic capabilities, i.e. strategic thinking capability, strategic processes, strategic time, etc., have atrophied. Executives struggle to negotiate greater management discretion from ownership and lack the experience and capability needed to utilize it effectively once they get it. If this leads to struggle and failure, ownership is forced to recruit leaders who already know how to get and exercise greater discretion.

Leaders who lack the experience and capability to create management discretion often lack the ability to fight against a board that inappropriately drives its executives into the weeds. I've seen executive teams so buried under tactical (often nonsensical) board demands that they can't spare five minutes for strategic thought.

If rising VUCA has increased the need for greater managerial discretion in your role as an executive and you're not positively reacting to this need, your effectiveness (and perhaps your job) is in jeopardy.

How groups push you into the weeds

A number of unintended consequences associated with groups and teams conspire to rob executives of strategic time.

First, executives are members of senior teams and leaders of departmental/functional teams. Because they're directly accountable for the latter – as the adage goes, there's 'one throat to choke' – they put their primary focus there, unintentionally drawing them into lower-level problems.

Second, organizational life naturally places us in many different relationships, each with its own expectations for how we should behave. However, some groups have more meaning to us than others, because we closely identify with their primary values, norms, interests, behaviors, etc. When asked to engage in behaviors inconsistent with those groups, we resist, even when the behaviors are logical and good for us. In fact, group allegiance is more important to influencing beliefs and directing behavior than science or facts.(13) Because many executives tend to identify more with the departmental and/or functional group they lead than with their senior teams, they're drawn to the lower-level problems those groups are working on.

Third, many departmental and functional groups (and some CEOs) tend to equate 'leadership effectiveness' with expertise in a technical and functional field – they don't respect executives who aren't experts in their field. As a result, many executives focus on lower-level problems because they believe the loss of technical, functional or project management skills will reduce their standing in the eyes of those they lead. It's a real concern. In my recent strategic time survey, 25% of executives said this perception is a personal barrier to their making strategic time.

Fourth, many executives primarily see themselves as advocates for the technical and functional teams they lead (their people do as well) and honoring that responsibility means staying intimately engaged with the lower-level problems faced by their people.

Finally, about 60% of executives consider their senior team to be ineffective,(14) a situation many find difficult to change. However, they do control the effectiveness of teams they lead, another reason to gravitate to the lower-level problems they're dealing with.

Executives have strong bonds to the groups and teams they lead. However, their primary allegiance does not lie there, instead it lies with the most senior organizational team they belong to. For instance, the primary allegiance of a CFO and every other senior team member is to the senior executive team, not to the teams they lead. To honor that responsibility, they must make the strategic time needed to focus on the highest-level problems the senior team's facing.

How poor strategy development pushes you into the weeds

In Chapter 2, we talked about how higher VUCA is forcing organizations to move from a 'strategic planning' mindset to a 'strategic thinking' one.

However, evidence suggests the need to improve the way executives develop and execute strategy goes beyond increased environmental disruption – dissatisfaction with the way it's been done for years is already high. For instance, only 2% of executives are confident they'll achieve 80–100% of their strategic objectives.[15]

In addition, translating strategy into executable plans remains a significant problem. Less than a third of senior executives' direct reports say that they clearly understand the connection between their work and corporate strategy and less than 20% of frontline supervisors and team leaders do.[16]

This data jives with my own experience. Most senior executive teams don't have recently updated strategic plans, and don't regularly or constructively discuss key high-level organizational elements like direction, strategy, operating model, leadership, and culture.

Ideally, this situation should stimulate more strategic thinking because it's clearly needed. However, it inadvertently has the opposite effect. A single executive can't affect organizational strategy on their own, so when there isn't a working structure of processes that translates strategic thinking into collective strategic dialogue, intention and action, executives don't see the benefit of strategic time.

If this sounds like you and your organization, this inattention to a workable strategic planning process should be the first thing you correct with the strategic time you make.

How the perception of politics pushes you into the weeds

The dictionary defines politics as activities associated with the debate or conflict among individuals having or hoping to achieve power. However, I think the definition advanced by Harold Lasswell is more succinct, 'Who gets what, when, how.'

In other words, politics is ultimately a fight for the allocation of resources – capital, authority, and people among others – and is an essential part of an executive's role, particularly at senior organizational levels. Unfortunately, politics has a bad name in many organizations because many executives consider it unethical – something you engage in when you can't get ahead more honestly.

In addition, many executives are afraid of political activity. In a survey of 116 CEOs, being politically attacked by colleagues was a significant fear. [(17)] I've personally witnessed the detrimental impact political power can have on groups/teams. For example, everyone on a senior team wants to focus on highest-level problems except one or two politically powerful members who keep the whole group stuck in the weeds – others go along out of fear of having that power turned against them.

This distaste and fear is real for many executives, prompts them to ignore the development of their own influencing capability, and discourages them from engaging in behavior perceived as overtly political by others. Research by Deloitte's leadership practice shows influencing is the least developed 'mental model' for most executives.[(18)]

However, without making the strategic time needed to understand the political landscape inside and outside the organization, build influencing skills to forge key relationships, take actions that build leverage, and persuade/negotiate effectively – all very time consuming activities

– you lack the ability needed to protect yourself and your department from more politically skilled colleagues.

How fear pushes you into the weeds

As an executive, it's natural to have fears. For instance, even successful learning experiences can create discomfort and anxiety. However, fear – an unpleasant emotion caused by a belief that someone or something is dangerous, likely to cause pain, or is a threat – elicits a stronger fight, flight, or freeze response.

Fear has benefits. If people don't feel fear, they might not protect themselves from legitimate threats because they don't step back from risky or dangerous situations where life, career, family, self-identity, etc., might be threatened.

Many executives encounter fear when they take on a new role because they're suddenly accountable for meeting expectations in a situation they're unfamiliar with, i.e. a new organization, culture, people, level of problem difficulty, etc. Fear's natural because first impressions matter so much – the first 100 days in a new executive role really do form lasting memories in others. [(19)]

As a result, many new executives focus on what's familiar in search of early wins, usually lower-level problems like the ones they've successfully solved in the past. Unfortunately, this inadvertently diverts them from more strategic initiatives with higher future value.

Fear is also familiar to many experienced, highly competent executives because most are susceptible to impostor syndrome – a persistent inability to believe one's success is deserved and legitimately earned. In a survey of 116 CEOs, impostor syndrome was identified as their greatest fear.[(17)]

It often manifests as low-grade discomfort or anxiety – people have a sense they'll eventually be found out as frauds or impostors – or can be a full-blown crisis of confidence. Many senior executives say it holds them back from tackling some particularly tough problems, because failure may reinforce their lack of self-belief and/or expose their incompetence.

Finally, VUCA may exacerbate fear and anxiety. Even though executives are comfortable with elevated risk compared to the general population,[18] the anxiety associated with regularly facing highest-level problems in disruptive environments can reduce coping ability over time.

For instance, I asked a COO succession candidate in a global public company what the strain of the top job might mean for him. He replied, 'I have no doubt I can do the job well if the stress doesn't kill me.'

Make no mistake, high VUCA produces higher risk for organizations and the executives that lead them. Reid Hoffman, the former COO of PayPal, maintains that strategy used to be like playing chess – the rules were relatively stable and understandable. Now, strategy is like walking through a minefield in the fog, and fear is a pre-condition of the role.[20]

It's the rare executive that doesn't encounter fear, especially as VUCA rises (you are not alone). Don't let it push you into the weeds.

How dysfunctional teams and meetings push you into the weeds

We've mentioned previously that highest-level problems are often so difficult – so Complex or Wicked – that solving them successfully involves the use of teams.

Unfortunately, many teams and their meetings are dysfunctional. In a recent survey, less than 40% of executives felt that their teams were performing effectively.[14] Almost 75% of meeting attendees report losing time to poorly organized meetings, and almost 50% say that bad meetings rob them of time to do more important things, creating more confusion than they resolve.[21]

I could cite many other studies, but I bet you know how pervasive this issue is from bitter experience – teams aren't focused on the right problems or lack the diversity, knowledge, and processes needed to deal with highest-level problems. Meetings lack purpose, agendas are poorly managed, and inconsistent attendance, electronic distractions, inattention, and poor preparation impede productivity.

How do bad teams and bad meetings inadvertently drive executives into the weeds?

For starters, most executive team members would rather be anywhere than interacting with dysfunctional teams and meetings so they mentally (and sometimes physically) check out – they focus on other problems, even when they're lower-level ones.

Bad teams or meetings focus on the wrong problems, usually working a full level of problem difficulty lower than they should. They also produce bad decisions, bogging others down in an avalanche of avoidable Tame problems as they're executed.

Badly managed executive team meetings are a notorious source of organizational ineffectiveness. Since executives spend 50–65% of their time in them, they're as big a strategic time killer as you'll find.

How a perceived lack of control keeps you in the weeds

In my strategic time survey, we asked executives whether they felt that making strategic time was within their control, and almost half said it wasn't. They see their lack of strategic time as the result of outside forces that they can't control, such as culture, policies, processes, etc.

This is significant because our sense of control over any situation has a significant impact on our ability to affect change. Many studies have confirmed that, as perceived control over a situation drops, so does the confidence, creativity, drive, and problem-solving capability needed to prevail. As a result, if you don't feel that you can alter the forces that drive executives into the weeds, you won't begin to confront them.

It's somewhat ironic that so many executives feel this way because they control the organizational forces that block them – as long as they've negotiated sufficient managerial discretion, they have the authority to change almost everything over time, including their ability to make strategic time.

There is no question that many barriers impede an executive's ability to make strategic time, but in the end, it really comes down to a personal choice – confront the barriers or stay in the weeds.

How lack of talent development pushes you into the weeds

When I ask executives why they're working on lower-level problems, the number one reason they cite is, 'I can't delegate difficult problems to my direct reports because they can't handle them.' In other words, they're in the weeds because others are stopping them from elevating to higher-level problems.

It's a frustrating response because it's difficult to know whether it's true – the executive may simply be an ineffective delegator. It's also frustrating because it implies that their inability to delegate is the direct report's fault. However, ensuring direct reports are capable to take on problems delegated to them is the responsibility of the executive.

Ineffective direct reports are usually the result of failure in two areas of executive responsibility: performance management and talent development. As a result, many executives find themselves in a circular process that exacerbates the problem: little to no strategic time leads to suboptimal talent and performance management, which leads to direct reports who can't elevate as needed, which leads to little to no strategic time.

The way out – make the strategic time needed to optimize performance and talent management, and before long you'll have direct reports more than capable of helping you elevate. Without doing so, you'll have the same problem two years from now.

How change and disruption push you into the weeds

In a world of rising change and disruption, it's easy to forget just how time consuming change truly is. Making a change requires reflection and design of the change, approvals to make the change happen, the retirement of old practices, retraining and learning of new practices, etc. – and a repeat of all of this when the change doesn't deliver desired results. The more strategic the change, the more organizational disruption is created. For example, a policy change affecting two departments might impact 20 people while a significant change in organizational direction and/or strategy might impact everyone.

Perversely, rising VUCA and disruption make it much harder to find the strategic time needed to effectively combat them.

Conclusion

Logging about 3000 hours per year, the typical executive works long hours, longer than almost all other organizational employees. Meetings, interactions with others, dealing with information, and managing people put them in constant demand to a wide variety of stakeholders. They know they need more strategic time to be effective and know they're not making enough of it. For many, changing that situation isn't about time-saving tools and techniques, it's about confronting and overcoming the barriers – many the result of unintended circumstances – that consistently push them into the weeds.

Topics we covered in Chapter 4 – What prevents executives from making and maintaining strategic time?

Topic	Page
• It's not for a lack of time and effort	45
• Meetings	47
• Interaction with others	47
• Dealing with information	48
• Performance management and people development	48
• What the data tells me	49
• It's not all about time-saving tools and techniques	49
• Getting out of the weeds is a change challenge	50
• How 'I'm not worth it' pushes you into the weeds	52
• How performance expectations push you into the weeds	52
• How 'Look, I'm urgent and busy' pushes you into the weeds	54
• How low management discretion pushes you into the weeds	54
• How groups push you into the weeds	56
• How poor strategy development pushes you into the weeds	57
• How the perception of politics pushes you into the weeds	58
• How fear pushes you into the weeds	59
• How dysfunctional teams and meetings push you into the weeds	60
• How a perceived lack of control keeps you in the weeds	61
• How lack of talent development pushes you into the weeds	61
• How change and disruption push you into the weeds	62
• Conclusion	62

5

HOW DO EXECUTIVES EFFECTIVELY MAKE AND MAINTAIN STRATEGIC TIME?

'Well, the first rule is that you can't really know anything if you just remember isolated facts and try and bang'em back… you've got to have models in your head and you've got to array your experience, both vicarious and direct, on this latticework of models.' – *Charlie Munger*

Introduction

IN CHAPTER 4, I suggested that making strategic time is primarily a change challenge, and forming a strong intention to change and taking action right away are two key steps to making change happen.

I also suggested many barriers are unintended consequences of other factors/decisions that inevitably arise for any executive, and I hope you've identified some barriers that may have gotten in your way in the past and committed to overcoming them. In Chapter 5, we turn our attention to taking action.

Flowing through the airport

There's a scene in the movie *Up In the Air*, where George Clooney's character 'teaches' a new colleague how to flow quickly through airport security because his travel experience allows him to anticipate bottlenecks she can't see. I get it because my own (significant) travel experience has provided me similar 'wisdom', getting me from my hotel room to my plane seat as fast and efficiently as possible.

There's lots to think about as you depart a city, but experience has taught me that only four things truly matter: a) getting to the airport; b) getting your boarding pass; c) getting through security; and d) getting through the boarding gate. Knowing everything else is superfluous, I can focus on developing a host of tactics for dealing with each of these four things.

Here's how I know it works. When I travel with my wife, she's constantly pleading, 'Will you please slow down, we're not in a hurry.' I'm not in a hurry either, it's just that I'm naturally making choices that increase my speed and efficiency. I'm an 'expert' at flight departures, and like all experts, I'm able to make informed actions that lead to successes quicker than non-experts because I have a well-developed 'departures' mental model. [(1)]

Anyone can build their expertise in anything – including making strategic time – by building an effective mental model.

Focus on four things

Most executives know dozens of different ideas for saving and managing time. Despite that wealth of knowledge, most don't create the strategic time they need.

After all, an overabundance of ideas isn't always a benefit – 'choice overload' is the term psychologists use to describe how too much information makes it harder to decide what to do, so we often don't do anything – we become immobilized. Besides, executives don't have time for experimentation, so they don't want to take actions that might not yield good value.

Research shows that one of the most effective ways to stimulate productive action is to provide people with a mental model or schema. A mental model is a simple cognitive framework or concept that helps us organize and access knowledge.

We naturally develop mental models for almost every activity we engage in. For example, 'social' models help us understand how people behave, 'event' models help us act appropriately in different social settings, 'travel' models (like mine) help us move efficiently as we move from place to place, etc.

As it relates to learning new behaviors and stimulating action, models have many advantages. For instance, they help us quickly focus on what is most important in any situation by directing our attention to the most essential elements. Models assist recall because they logically sort knowledge into groupings and hierarchies based on their value to us in a given situation. This sorting accelerates capability development because new knowledge is added to those groupings as we learn.

Based on my research and dialogue with many executives, I've developed a simple model/schema for making strategic time. It turns out those executives who are particularly skilled at staying out of the weeds consistently focus on four simple things:

- Allocate time – they carefully consider and prioritize where they need to spend their time and ensure as much time as possible is made available for those priorities, i.e. they allocate specific times in their schedule and calendar for strategic thinking;

- Monitor time – they regularly measure where their time is going to ensure priorities are being maintained and/or make adjustments as soon as possible when they're not, i.e. they regularly check their calendar to ensure time they've allotted to priorities is being honored;

- Create time – they consider every method, tool and technique possible to create strategic time in their calendars and regularly utilize as many as possible, i.e. they read, consult with others, etc. so their repository of information is being constantly expanded; and

- Manage time – they recognize time as one of an organization's most valuable resources and endeavor to make management decisions that create strategic time for themselves and others and/or prevent the erosion of time, i.e. when considering a change to an established process, they evaluate the implications it will have on time.

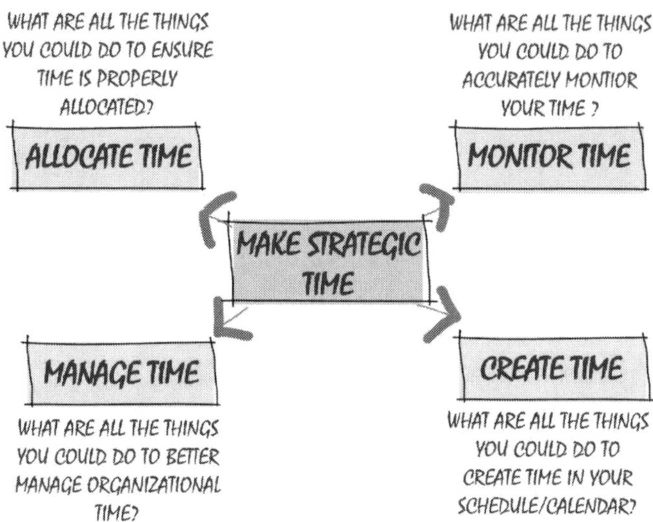

As you can see this simple model isn't 'rocket science' – hopefully you instantly recognize it and have already developed tools and techniques applicable to each element. What we're going to do for the rest of the book is use this model to reinforce and supplement what you already know and do.

Focus on all four things all the time

In addition to helping us focus on what's most important in any situation, mental models remind us that maximum effectiveness demands a focus on the full model all the time – focusing your attention on most elements but leaving one element under-used weakens the whole model.

You can see the logic in this by looking at a few different scenarios. For instance, in this first scenario an executive does a great job allocating, creating and managing time. However, over the course of a few months, distractions and operational pressures inevitably impinge on their calendar. Lower-level problems they shouldn't be associated with – in the form of projects and meetings – slip into their calendar and the time they had allocated to priorities collapses. By not consciously monitoring how they're tracking time against their allocations, they backslide. In fact, executives who regularly maintain strategic time warn that it's only careful attention to monitoring that tells them they're off-track and forces them back on the rails.

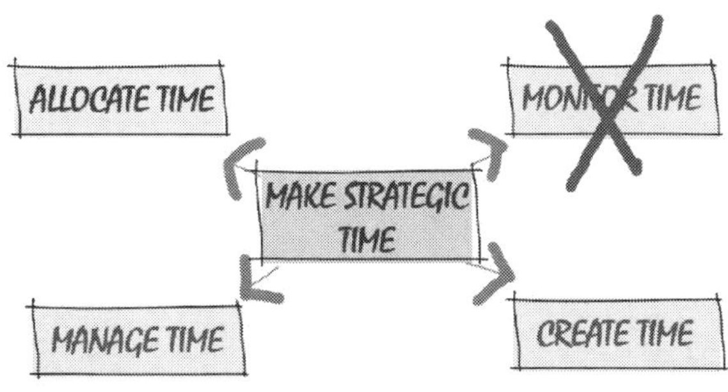

In this second scenario, a senior executive does a great job of allocating, monitoring, and creating their own time, successfully making the time they need for highest-level priorities. However, their decisions are creating organizational churn and change without fully considering the negative impact it has on the focus and productivity of others. The strategic time they've made is offset by the time eroded by their decisions.

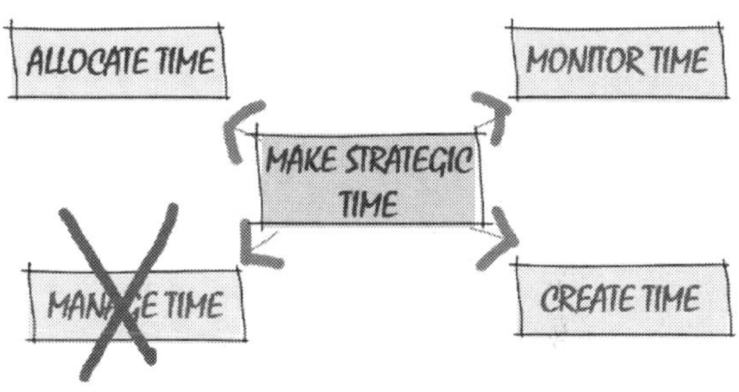

For a number of reasons, many executives don't consider the implications change has on time. Any big change demands the time of many people for exploration, decision-making, aligning the organization, and implementation. In addition, the decision likely shifts policies, procedures, processes, and practices affecting many others. It may also shift reporting lines and job roles that require retraining for all impacted, mothballing the practices the change has created (they often die very reluctantly), course correcting as change evolves through implementation, etc. Furthermore, any big change requires executive oversight – change (even when it's a great idea or inevitable) has the potential to drag you and many others deep into the weeds.

In this third scenario, another executive diligently allocates the time they need for working on highest-level problems, has a good sense for how they're spending their time, and is careful about the impact their decisions have on the organization's use of time. However, they can't create the time needed to maintain a focus on their priorities. Their calendar is constantly blocked, they run frantically from one fire to another, bad meetings constantly erode personal productivity, and they're overloaded with irrelevant information, email communications, etc. They know exactly what they'd do if they could make strategic time but they just can't get there.

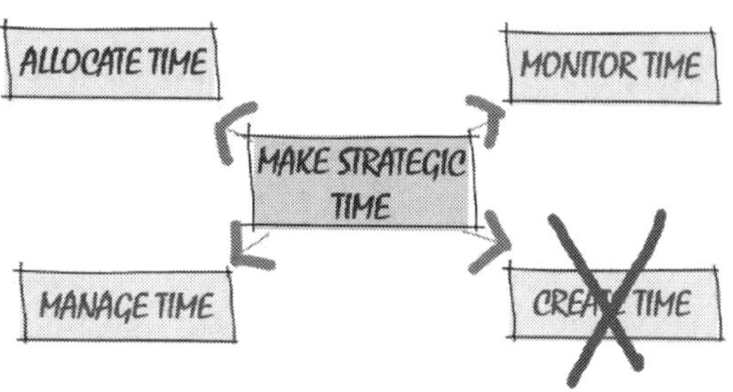

In this final scenario, an executive doesn't feel a strong impetus for making strategic time because they haven't allocated time for strategic priorities. As a result, they're content to let others control their focus and time because doing so seems to keep everyone happy. This approach hasn't stopped their promotion up through their department, and they don't see why it won't work as an executive. Besides, even when they've considered setting clear strategic priorities, they're not sure it's what their boss wants them to do, and strategic projects prevent them delivering on those responsibilities they already have.

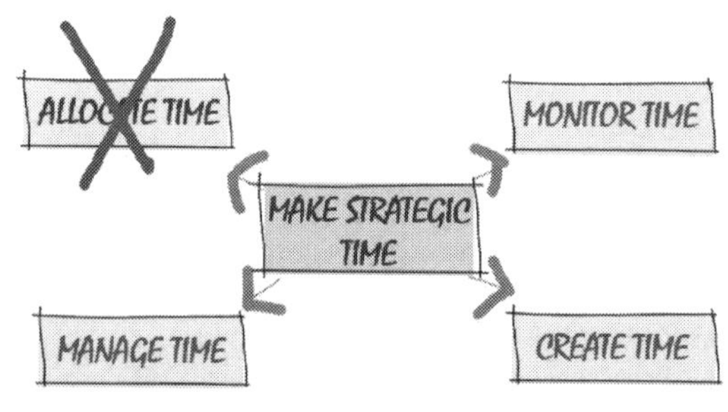

I provide these simple scenarios for one reason – effectively making strategic time demands regular attention to all four elements in the model, all of the time. Executives might have a rock-solid intention for making strategic time – they understand it's imperative if they're to fulfill their executive responsibilities for strategic development and execution. However, without regular attention to the allocation, monitoring, creation, and management of time, those intentions may not last any longer than a typical New Year's resolution.

Alternatives are important

Another principle for making mental models or schemas work effectively is to ensure that each element in the schema has multiple choices or alternatives for taking action.

For example, imagine you want to create an extra three to four hours a week for strategic thinking and you're familiar with two tactics; reduce meeting time, and improve the agenda for every meeting you attend. However, if you can't drop any meetings because they're organized by people more senior than you and your suggestions to improve agendas have been ignored, you're out of luck.

However, as you'll see in Chapter 8, there are dozens of alternate ways to create time, and the more you use, the greater your likelihood of success. That's why I encourage executives to take every opportunity they can to swap ideas with other executives. For example ask, 'When it comes to allocating/prioritizing time for strategic thinking, what works best for you?'

I also recommend you maintain a paper or electronic logbook of the best ideas associated with all four elements in the model so that when current tactics aren't working, you can quickly access alternatives. In addition, I've provided a table at the end of each chapter outlining the topics covered and the page you can find them on - put a check mark next to those you may want to implement.

Start right away or sooner

Another key to making mental models work effectively is to start using them as soon as possible. Remember the Conscious Competence Model

– no tactic for making strategic time will work unless it's put into practice, otherwise it simply remains a concept or idea. The experience we gain through practice transforms it into working knowledge – knowledge we've learned to apply effectively in our specific work circumstances.

I feel so strongly about this I can offer a guarantee – if you don't put any of the concepts/ideas/tactics from this book into practice, I guarantee the cost of the book and (much more significantly) the time it took you to read it will be a waste of time and money (unfortunately, this is not a money-back guarantee).

As such, I strongly recommend you begin making strategic time immediately, starting with the element that will provide maximum impact for you as soon as possible. A schema is not a step-by-step process – you can apply the elements in any order that serves you best. Having said that, most of my clients start by creating time. It's often the easiest to apply, provides immediate relief, and carves out time you can use to plan how you'll tackle the other elements.

When I help executives make strategic time, they usually come to me frustrated and overwhelmed with their current schedule – they want help urgently. Here's how a typical dialogue might unfold:

> I begin by saying, 'You sound pretty frustrated. Is there an opportunity to create some time right now?'
>
> They usually answer, 'Yes.'
>
> 'Great, what will you do?'
>
> 'I'm going to stop attending this series of meetings. They're a waste of my time.' (A sense of relief as they admit this to themselves.)
>
> 'Sounds good. What do you need to do to stop them?'
>
> 'I'll email the chairperson. They're not going to like it, but it should work.' (a slight sense of doubt slips in.)
>
> 'What would work better, an email or a face-to-face conversation?'
>
> 'Face-to-face.' (The prospect of a face-to-face is discouraging because it means investing more time.)

'OK, when will you do this?'

'I have to set it up. I can find time to do that on Thursday.' (Two to three days from now.)

'Can you find time to set it up this afternoon?'

'Sure, I can carve out a few minutes.'

'Great, can you set the meeting for Thursday?'

'Yes, pretty sure I can.'

'Great. This is going to give you back at least an hour a week. Can you pop me a quick text end of day Thursday to let me know how it went?'

'Sure.'

This might feel rigid and pedantic, however, the likelihood of change increases dramatically when we process doubts and objections and get into action (before good intentions fade).

For our executive, this conversation produces 60 minutes of strategic thinking time a week (not a lot but a good start), the relief that comes from a simple plan of action, and a drop in frustration. Not bad for a minute of effort.

You already know how to do this

I mentioned earlier that the model I propose for making strategic time is not rocket science. In fact, you might look at it and think 'I already know this.' Moreover, you probably do. After all, you've been managing time since childhood and your successful career to date implies considerable success with time management.

However, the combination of rising VUCA, the difficulty of highest-level problems, the severe time challenges the executive role naturally produces, and the barriers organizational life inadvertently create mean executive strategic time is the hardest time to make.

This model is my attempt to supplement and support your current knowledge and success with something that might provide a bit more guidance.

Conclusion

Models are proven to accelerate learning, improve recall, and facilitate action. Executives with a good track-record for staying out of the weeds do so by keeping four elements top of mind: allocating, monitoring, creating, and managing time. They ensure they regularly pay attention to all four elements, constantly create new and alternate ways of deploying each element, get into action ASAP to build momentum before good intentions fade, and never stop learning/introducing new ways to make strategic time.

Topics we covered in Chapter 5 – How do executives effectively make and maintain strategic time?

Topic	Page
• Introduction	65
• Flowing through the airport	66
• Focus on four things	66
• Focus on all four things all the time	68
• Alternatives are important	71
• Start right away or sooner	71
• You already know how to do this	73
• Conclusion	74

6

ALLOCATE STRATEGIC TIME – SPOT THE HIGH GROUND

'The trick is to make yourself an instrument of your own policy'. – Norman Mailer

Introduction

ALLOCATION IS THE process of distributing resources (in this case, time) to specific duties or areas of responsibility based on priorities you've set for yourself.

It's not as easy as it sounds. Anyone who's tried to make and maintain New Year's resolutions knows how hard it can be to set a goal for the future, allocate time to achieve it, and systematically make their way there – apparently, over 80% fail. [1]

Just as asset allocation is a strategy for selecting a mix of investments to achieve financial goals, time allocation is a strategy for investing time that will help you advance towards significant organizational and career goals – it's about making time that's most meaningful to you and your organization.

For executives, I believe optimum time allocation is where unique, personal attributes are directed to areas that materially affect their capacity to obtain desired organizational and career results.

For the sake of their career, people have a personal responsibility to themselves to allocate time to those areas that take full advantage of their unique skills and capabilities. As executives, people have a fiduciary responsibility to allocate time to strategic development and execution.

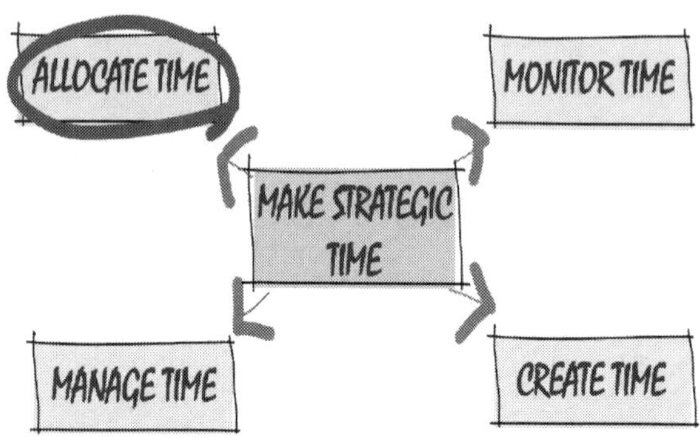

No one wins when executives 'fritter themselves away operating.'[(2)] Time allocation is an effort to resist the pull of the weeds through conscious intention – what the Greeks called 'the time of human opportunity'. It's doable. After all, research has shown executives spend about 40% of their time on unsatisfactory and unfulfilling discretionary events that could be dropped, delegated or redesigned with little impact on effectiveness.[(3)]

Strategic time is time dedicated to the strategic priorities that create maximum organizational and personal value. We use strategic time to prepare for a better future.

When was the last time you paused, identified the three to five most meaningful areas/domains in your life and work, and truly committed a percentage of your time and energy there?

As Bonnie Ware's palliative care patients have come to learn (discussed in Chapter 4), time is a finite resource – we all get a little over 119 waking hours a week and the power to exercise a choice: to consciously allocate as much of them as possible to the actualization of our talent, potential, aspirations, and executive responsibilities, or to something else.

Allocate strategic time – guiding principles

Before looking at time allocation strategies and tactics, let's outline a few principles to help guide us.

- Know where you're trying to go – sustain an image of a future state – yours and the organization's – so the time you allocate is for the sake of taking you there;

- Less is more – focus on two to three high-level aspirations/areas of priority that best push you toward your desired future state, because 20% of action typically accounts for 80% of results;

- Always be consciously prioritizing – whenever you choose one activity over another, whether you know it or not, you've prioritized. As much as possible, make conscious choices that serve your priorities, not someone else's; and

- There's always an opportunity cost – time is a finite resource, and when you say yes to something that doesn't match your priorities, you're saying no to something else that might.

How do you see yourself?

Before you think about allocating your time, I have a serious question for you. Are you a **very effective** executive?

Please take a minute to reflect on this. Do you see yourself as a very effective executive, a moderately effective one, an overwhelmed 'stuck in the weeds' one, a functional expert, a team leader? Please consider this because how we see ourselves has a significant (usually unconscious) impact on our choices and behaviors.

This is because our perspective of ourselves directly impacts our thoughts, feelings, and emotions and influences our behaviors – what we say or do. When we perceive a situation from the perspective of a 'very effective' executive, we're more likely to think, do and say things a very effective executive would think, say and do. Subsequently, we perceive the positive impact these behaviors have on the situations we find ourselves in, and our perspective as a very effective executive is strengthened. It's a virtuous circle.

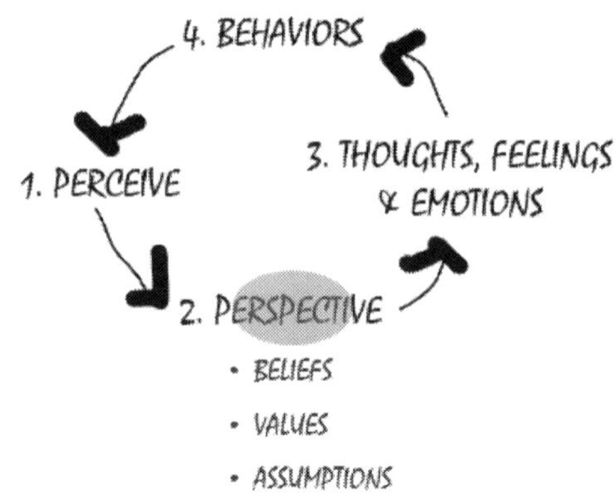

Very effective executives see themselves as organizational leaders responsible for increasing shareholder and stakeholder value through the development and execution of sound strategy. To do this, they must allocate the strategic time needed to do it well. And when they do, they're being an effective executive.

When you see yourself as 'very effective', you tend to do the things 'very effective' people do (and vice versa). When you see yourself as something other than a very effective executive, i.e. a departmental leader, a technical expert, someone who's not strategic, etc., it's little wonder you spend time focused on lower-level problems – that's what those folks do.

Why do you want to make strategic time?

This book's first two chapters present logical reasons why executives must make strategic time. Essentially, VUCA causes organizations to struggle and fail because highest-level problems become more difficult and executives can't effectively solve them – can't do their job – without strategic time.

While this represents my logic for making strategic time, yours might be completely different. Personal decisions don't need to be logical, spring from organizational responsibilities, or be significant to anyone but you.

They just need to be personally compelling, because they're the emotional fuel needed to overcome the forces driving you into the weeds.

For instance, you might want to make strategic time because you're fed-up with life on the 'treadmill of work existence', or you're suddenly infused with the realization you can reach higher than you ever thought possible. Alternatively, you and/or your organization have a bold new vision for the future. Or things might be failing right now and making strategic time is a last-ditch effort to create sustainable improvement or a personal opportunity to develop a path in an exciting new career direction.

Get beyond the surface – what are your intrinsic rewards for making strategic time? To get at foundational drivers, use a simple technique called The Five Whys (you can see an example below or consult your favorite internet search engine for more info).

The 5 Whys

1. Why is making strategic time important to you? Because it's key to a promotion.
2. Why is a promotion important to you? Because it means more money.
3. Why is more money important to you? Because it means more security for my family.
4. Why is more security for your family important to you? Because I never had security growing up.
5. Why is providing more security than you had as a child important to you? Because I want my kids to know anything's possible if you truly want to succeed.

I invite you to reflect deeply on why strategic time is truly important to you. Once you've found important personal reasons, write them down and revisit them a day, week, or month later to test whether they're still compelling. If they cease to be compelling, try this exercise again, because things shift and what inspires us in one moment might not work in another.

Envision a desired future state

Allocating time is essentially an intention (or promise to yourself) to spend future time on activities you've prioritized because they'll bring you closer to a desired future state.

This represents a challenge if you (or the organization) don't know where you want to go, i.e. there's a lack of clear direction and strategy. Under these circumstances, it's easy to see how some executives wind up working on someone else's priorities – their boss's, key stakeholders', their team's, etc. – rather than their own.

While I have sympathy for executives stuck on the treadmill of work and life, and at the risk of sounding judgmental (I'm not), the inability to make strategic time is a personal and organizational failure that has far-reaching implications for everyone around them.

Successful time allocation begins with a clear-headed analysis of where the organization is headed (we discussed the high-level organizational elements that support this in Chapter 2) – what it's trying to achieve in the long term combined with clarity about your own personal aspirations and goals. Where those two paths intersect is where you should allocate most of your time.

Here are seven questions that will help guide your consideration of how your time might be best allocated to priorities* – you don't need to use them all; choose the one or two that work best for you. Revisit the first six on a quarterly or half yearly basis so time allocations remain current, and revisit the seventh one whenever you feel like you're in the weeds:

- Why am I on the payroll – is what I'm doing right now the most important thing I've been hired to do? If my boss was watching me, what would I be doing differently from what I'm doing at this moment?

**Adapted from Brian Tracy and others.*

- Two hours per day – what if something happened that limited my ability to work to 10-12 hours a week? What would be the absolute best use of my time and energy now?

- Life goals – what am I trying to accomplish in my life – what are the directions and specific long-term objectives? How should I allocate my time to achieve my objectives?

- Highest value activities – since about 20% of my effort accounts for about 80% of the value I create, what three to four things must I work on to create the most value for the organization and/or myself?

- Key objectives – what are two to four goals that will make the biggest difference in my next performance review? What are the one or two things I have to hit out of the park? What are the one or two things I can't drop the ball on?

- Areas of greatest impact – what are those things in my life that might have the biggest impact on the most people? When I'm most passionate, confident, motivated and impactful with others, what am I doing?

- What should I be doing right now – right now, is this thing I'm working on, i.e. this meeting, relationship, information, etc. the best use of my time, or should I set this aside and reorient?

Executive teams need shared priorities

Most executive team members struggle to make strategic time because the full team itself hasn't established shared, high-level priorities. If this sounds like your team, ask yourself, 'What's the purpose of this team? What are the high-level objectives/priorities we must achieve for success?'

As much as possible, organizational priorities of individual executives should spring from the shared priorities established by their executive team. The time you allocate for your own work must include the time needed to advance the team's shared priorities.

In the absence of shared team priorities, team members do their own thing, including getting in the weeds.

Be clear about what you won't do

No one has time for everything, and saying yes to something inevitably means saying no to something else. As a result, it pays to consciously reflect on those things you don't enjoy – you're not good at them, they bring you little satisfaction and they don't tap into your unique capabilities – and decide you'll do as little of them as possible.

If your calendar/schedule is populated with things you don't want to do, start taking action to remove them. That might mean notifying someone, finding someone to take your place, etc. Going forward, when you're asked to do them, you'll say no unless you have absolutely no choice.

When people close the door to the things they don't want to do, they feel the relief that comes from removing a burden in their life – like an aching tooth that's finally fixed – and find more time for other more valuable endeavors. It also gives others the opportunity to pick up those things you abandon - they might love doing them. When that happens, no longer doing what you don't want to do makes at least two people happier and more productive.

Write priorities/time allocations down

A time allocation is essentially a goal – an intention or promise to yourself to meet an objective in the future. Research shows that future intentions/goals that are written down are much more likely to be realized.[4]

As it relates to written goals, people fall into three groups: the vast majority of people who don't make goals, a smaller group that do but don't write them down, and a very small minority that do write them down. Studies show this last group usually outperforms the other two.

It follows that the key to effective time allocation is writing them down. First, write down the reason(s) why the time allocation is so important to you, i.e. a promotion, long-term development, achievement of a personal or organizational goal, etc. Second, make the allocation measurable, i.e. x hours per week, day of the week and/or time of the day. Third, identify the steps you must take to achieve the allocations with deadlines for completion (Chapter 8 will help with this). Fourth, take action right away. Fifth, monitor progress regularly (Chapter 7 will help with this), and make adjustments that maintain allocations.

When time allocations aren't written down, you can't remind yourself of your commitments or monitor progress.

Remind yourself as often as possible

A big reason we fail to honor promises or intentions is we simply forget about them. As we're pulled into the weeds, it's natural to lose sight of important but less urgent things in our life.

One way to combat this is to make an association between symbols or objects and our intentions, similar to the way a wedding band reminds us of our commitment to our partner. Any symbol or object can be used to remind us of our intention to allocate time, as long as it's regularly visible, for example an object on your desk, a picture or poster, computer screen saver, etc.

Some people find symbols/objects lose their potency because they blend into the background over time. To combat this, make it something you deal with regularly, such as a pop-up reminder in your calendar or something placed in the middle of your desk so you have to move it to begin work in the morning. I have a 'Strategic Thinking' sticker on my laptop that's a very effective reminder.

Of course, there are now apps that will perform this function for you. An interesting one related to time is WeCroak – it sends five messages a day reminding you to make the most of your time on Earth because it's short.

Another idea I find very useful is to link an intention with a daily or weekly activity. For instance, as I make my bed every morning, I automatically do a mental check on how well my activities for the day align with my strategic time allocations.

Finally, perhaps the best example I've seen of an executive constantly reminding himself of time allocations was an individual who had installed full-height whiteboards on the walls of his office. He posted anything he wanted to keep top of mind, including quotes, ideas, timelines for significant projects, overarching goals, time allocations, etc. on two of the walls (the other two were for making notes during team meetings). It worked very well.

How much strategic time do you need to allocate?

In my strategic time survey, over 50% of respondents felt that they needed more than four additional hours per week dedicated to highest-level problem solving than they currently dedicate – so about an additional half day per week. That aligns with the anecdotal evidence from many executive coaching clients who invariably say they need at least an additional four to five hours a week of strategic thinking time to meet the strategic demands of their role.

However, I suspect most underestimate the time they need, because when executives refer to 'highest-level problems' they're usually referring to the highest-level problems their team is currently working on – which, based on my survey, are typically Complex and Tame in nature, with time spans of less than one-and-a-half years.

They're not referring to the big, Wicked problems – with time spans of three to seven years – they would likely encounter if they weren't drawn into operational issues and were spending more time truly thinking strategically about their environment.

The amount of time you need to allocate for strategic thinking on highest-level problems is unique to your circumstances. I've known some who dedicate more than 50% of their time while others spend 5% or less.

However, if you're spending less than five to six hours/week, you should consider increasing it or have a good reason for not doing so.

Allocate more 'high importance/low urgency' time

Many people use the 'Eisenhower Principle' when thinking about allocating time. It's named after President Eisenhower because it's said he used it to organize tasks and priorities.

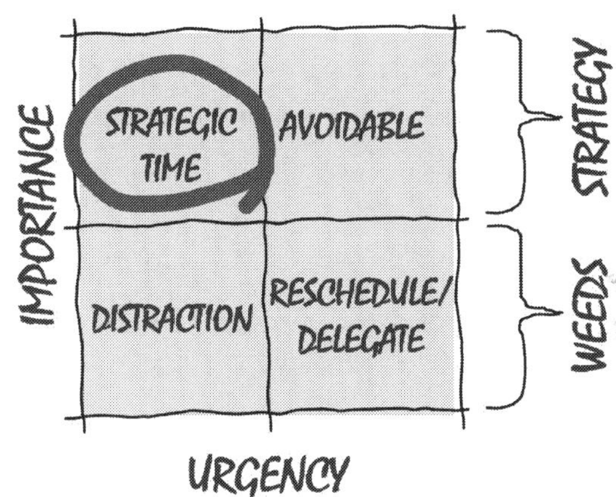

Important tasks and priorities are those that take us closer to our goals, and urgent ones demand our attention whether they support our goals or not. Important tasks are those that focus us on the high-level organizational elements discussed in Chapter 2 – organizational purpose, direction, strategy, operating model, leadership, culture, and operational oversight – urgent tasks are those that drive us into the weeds.

Arranged on a 2x2 matrix, we can see strategic time is where high importance/low urgency priorities usually reside. As much as possible, executives should avoid any contact whatsoever with low importance/low urgency tasks (lower left quadrant) as 99% of them are Tame distractions solvable by many others.

Low importance/high urgency tasks (lower right quadrant) are attractive to executives because their urgency makes them look more important than they are, for example a report your boss is screaming for you to deliver. Fight the temptation to engage actively and maintain an oversight or quality assurance role, delegating production to others and/or negotiate an extension to reduce urgency and your involvement.

High importance/high urgency tasks (upper right quadrant) are usually crises directly resulting from a lack of strategic time (upper left quadrant) and/or high VUCA – the result of strategic initiatives or environmental signals that didn't get the time they deserved when things were less urgent. In my work with senior teams, I've seen loads of executive time and energy dedicated to this quadrant – executives are stuck in a cycle of high-stakes reaction to events spinning out of control.

If that describes you, you're going to hate what comes next – the only way out is making more strategic time to work on high importance/low urgency tasks before they descend into avoidable crisis.

Ideally, how much of your schedule should be spent in each quadrant? If you can't achieve that allocation right now, what date do you intend to be there?

Allocate time based on time span

The Canadian psychologist Elliott Jaques used the phrase 'time span' to describe the amount of time, into the future, a specific role requires an individual to set a goal and plan for systematically reaching it.

Time spans vary considerably from role to role in organizations, for instance, a customer service representative may have a time span of one day. Their primary responsibility is to meet a series of goals, for example customer satisfaction rates, number of customers served, etc., over an eight-hour shift.

A director in the same organization may have a time span of one year – their primary responsibility is to meet a series of goals, such as a budget with revenue/sales targets, profit targets, employee engagement targets, etc., on an annual basis.

Finally, in the same organization, a senior executive may have a time span of three to five years (or longer) – their primary responsibility is to meet a series of more strategic goals, for example revenue/sales, profit, and market/geographic growth targets, over that longer time period.

Different roles have responsibility for initiatives with very different completion dates because organizational roles don't just describe what we're responsible for, they also describe what we're responsible for by a certain date or deadline (time span) to reflect the length of time it takes to implement a solution. The longer the time span, the 'bigger' and more difficult the role.

As a result, many executives allocate time according to the time span of their role. For instance, I worked with a CEO (of a relatively large organization) who recognized a series of ongoing, constantly evolving trends could negatively affect the organization in the future, and any initiatives aimed at addressing these trends successfully would likely take at least five years to implement given the scale of the solution and the size and nature of the organization. As a result, she determined the time span of her role was five years.

Because she was the only person focused on a five-year time span and the problems were so difficult, she allocated 85% of her time to thinking strategically about these highest-level problems. For instance, she ensured stakeholders she interrelated with had information that would help her understand and analyze this five-year time span. Conferences, books, other CEOs, regulators, etc. were regularly consulted for information and insights of what the future might hold, and 85% of her meeting time and interaction with others (inside and outside the organization) was on subjects pertaining to problems and initiatives five years into the future.

Furthermore, she composed her senior team with people capable of working three-year time spans, requiring them to spend 50% of their time thinking strategically about how the problems they worked on addressed the organization's highest-level problems.

Subsequently, those who reported directly to the members of her senior team focused on problems with one and two-year timespans. In this way, she ensured executives occupying key roles in the chain of command allocated time consistent with the time span of their role and focused on the highest-level problems at each level.

She also recognized the intention to maintain 85% of her time on important five-year problems would face constant pressure from more urgent, shorter-term ones. As a result, she reviewed her schedule every three months and removed anything impeding her longer-term plan (see more about monitoring time in Chapter 7). Executive team members were accountable for doing the same.

Finally, she evaluated talent based on their ability to make strategic time, knowing those who readily find time for highest-level problems are usually better at solving them than others. For the purpose of succession planning, she was on the lookout for those demonstrating the potential to work up to five-year time spans, providing them opportunities to develop that longer-term strategic thinking capability they would need when they assumed her role.

I believe time span is a key concept for executives to consider when allocating time because it relates nicely to the concept of highest-level problems. For instance, as a rough guide, you might envision time span lining up with the four levels of problem difficulty: Tame problems = time spans of one year or less; Complex problems = time spans of one to three years; Wicked problems = time spans of three to six years; and Extra Wicked problems = longer than six years. You might aim to allocate 10-20% of your time to problems with three to five-year time spans, knowing that by doing so, you'll likely be confronting Wicked problems.

Given the VUCA and disruption faced by your organization, what's the time span most appropriate for the CEO and other senior executives? What time span is most appropriate for your role? The minute you increase the time span of the problems you work on, you elevate your level of problem difficulty.

Allocate time based on inside/outside focus

In Chapter 1, I proposed the organizational life cycle might prompt executives to react differently to disruption, i.e. organizations in the Start-Up or High Growth phases might perceive disruption as an opportunity, while those in the Stable Growth or Stable Decline phases would likely perceive it as a threat to their market dominance.

One reason for these different perspectives is the tendency for executives in the first two phases to focus most of their attention outside their organizations scouring the market – a Prospecting strategy.[(6)] Because big disruptions come from the external environment they're focused on, these executives are more likely to see them coming and embrace them as opportunities.

However, once organizations have built sustainable growth, they begin to focus inside the organization – a Defender strategy[6] – building structures and mechanisms for sustaining success and losing focus on the external environment.

Research has shown that as VUCA rises, Prospecting strategies become more effective. This requires executives to prioritize more focus outside the organization. After all, organizational disruption starts with unhappy customers, not something occurring inside the organization. It's your relationship with your external environment, i.e. markets, competitors, etc. that determines your organization's vulnerability to disruption.

The amount of time you should allocate outside the organization is situational, however, if you don't specifically allocate the time necessary for effectively interacting with clients or customers, regulators, competitors, industry experts, other executives on not-for-profit boards, and other peer groups, you're not going to have the information you need to anticipate and deal successfully with highest-level problems.

This is why you need to determine how much of your time must be allocated to external activities versus internal ones. Remember, executives have more permission to represent the organization to outside customers and stakeholders than any other employee, so if they're not spending time doing it, it's probably not happening at all.

Pomodoro technique – conserving energy

An Italian developed the 'Pomodoro technique' [7] in the 1980s (it was named after a kitchen timer shaped like a tomato). The technique is based on studies showing that our motivation and ability to concentrate is higher when we work in short intervals interspersed with short breaks [8] because after 45–55 minutes, most of us suffer a drop in motivation and concentration.

The Pomodoro technique proposes we start any task by first allocating a specific length of time for completion, for example, we allot two hours to finalize the first draft of a report. Then, break that time into smaller intervals each followed by a short break to reignite motivation and concentration, for example, a three-hour time allotment might be broken up into six 30-minute segments.

I personally set the timer on my phone (or ask Siri to do it) to ring after 25 minutes, followed by a five-minute break. I then reset it for the same time and take another five-minute break when it rings. I repeat this process for the full three hours. As a result, for every 60 minutes I work 50 minutes (two and a half hours over the three-hour period). However, I find my productivity remains much higher over the entire three-hour time allotment. I have also found this technique keeps groups and teams engaged with difficult problems much fresher than breaking for 20 minutes every two hours (a typical sequence for most groups).

The ideal length and sequence of time segments varies from person to person and group to group. In addition, resist the temptation to ignore a break because you're 'on a roll'. After a five-minute break, I find I'm able to pick right up where I've left off with fresh energy and (often) a new perspective.

An added benefit – using a timer consistently has been shown to increase our sense of time and makes us better at estimating how much time to allocate to different tasks.

Allocate time based on key functions

As you rise in an organization and take on responsibilities with increased levels of problem difficulty, the best way of allocating time will change with new responsibilities.

Fortunately, many other executives have been in roles similar to yours and have determined – usually through trial and error – the best ways to allocate time for specific roles and responsibilities.

In a recent interview, the author of *Good to Great*, Jim Collins, talked about his start as a fresh, new academic and author.[(9)] He found himself pulled in multiple directions and wasn't sure how to best allocate time in this new role, so he approached other academic/authors for ideas.

They suggested he allocate his time to three key functions. First, creating content, i.e. research, reflection, design, writing, re-writing, etc. Because the quality of his teaching and books relies on the quality of his content, he allocates 50% of his time to this function.

Second, teaching, i.e. classroom, interaction with students outside the classroom, interaction with colleagues, etc. Because the point of his content is to educate, and teaching is such a rich source of new ideas, he allocates 30% of his time to this function.

Finally, all other activities, i.e. everything else not included in these first two functions, is assigned to an 'other' category; time he must invest to ensure that the other two functions thrive. He'd like to allocate less time here, but finds it takes 20% of his time.

An acknowledged expert in the consulting field, Alan Weiss, proposes another great example of using key functions to allocate time. He suggests allocating available time against four separate but interrelated functions: attracting work, converting opportunities to contracts, delivering on the contract, and expanding your footprint with the client to solidify your position. By mapping a current allocation to one you desire, you immediately see where a change in focus needs to happen.

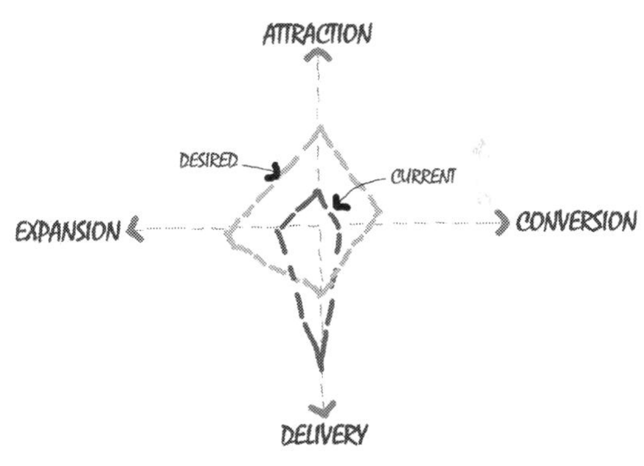

Similarly, Marilyn Paul and David Peter Stroh[(10)] propose leaders allocate their time against four leadership functions: guide (mobilize commitment, and strategize); think (think strategically); relate (build relationships and community); and do (organize for action).

I admire all these methods because together they exemplify three best practices for allocating strategic time. First, they're flexibly adaptable to many fields of endeavor. For instance, the allocations proposed by Alan Weiss were developed for consulting but are certainly applicable to sales, account management, relationship development, etc.

Second, they demonstrate the power of experts to cut through all the noise and focus on what's truly important.

Third, they keep things simple – in my experience with executives,

80% of their responsibilities neatly roll up into three or four categories, and anything that doesn't can be thrown into an 'other' category.

Maintain control of your top priorities

According to the dictionary, a priority is a thing regarded more important than other things. However, as business writer Karen Martin says, 'When everything is a priority, nothing is a priority.'

There are many reasons why people lose sight of priorities – they're not clear about them in the first place, they allow non-priorities to overtake them, or they have too many. Too many priorities combined with too little strategic time is a recipe for failure.

How many priorities is the right amount? It varies from person to person, because variables like productivity, amount of strategic time available, etc. vary. However, any more than three priorities should prompt the question, 'Am I being discerning enough?'

Once clear on a manageable number, don't add a new priority unless you're willing to drop an existing one. This recognizes that priorities change over time, maintains focus on what's most important, and guards against taking on more than you can handle.

Always have an active, significant strategic priority

In my coaching with executives, I've met many who don't have any strategic priorities because the nature of their responsibilities, i.e. highly technical roles serving specific internal or external clients, keeps them buried in the weeds.

They're frustrated because they see how more strategic approaches would yield greater efficiency and effectiveness, but they don't have the mandate, expertise, or time needed to develop and implement changes.

I encourage them to take the following steps. First, ask yourself, 'What are the two biggest opportunities to add significant new value to my clients?' Second, meet separately with your boss and a few of your clients and ask the same question. Third, reflect on the information collected, and consider a few potential initiatives that bring the most value to all concerned. Fourth, go to your boss and pitch the initiatives with the intention of identifying one he or she is prepared to support. Finally, prepare a plan for moving the initiative forward, including actions (with deadlines) required to make strategic time.

If strategic thinking is good for your career and the organization, but you're not currently being given opportunities to make time for it, this is a great way to demonstrate initiative and take control. When you've delivered successfully on this initiative, be immediately open to another.

Unfortunately, I've also worked with executives who have lost touch with significant strategic initiatives they're responsible for delivering; they're not working on them, can't accurately relate the name, purpose, and goals of the initiatives, and are missing deadlines.

It's a clear sign that they're not making strategic time, and there's nothing to do but personally recommit to the initiative or arrange to have it given to an executive who can tackle it more effectively.

Always work to a deadline

Few things help maintain time allocations better than deadlines, because they strengthen attention to a task and resolve.

Keep the deadlines challenging and tight. Remember the adage, 'Time expands to fill the time allotted.' Give yourself 10 days to complete a task that should take five days, and you'll increase the work to fill the 10 days. To stimulate creativity (there's evidence the constraint of a tight timeline increases creativity)[11] and productivity, work to a four-day deadline instead.

Use deadlines to overcome resistance. For instance, if you're struggling to keep key stakeholders or colleagues engaged with a strategic initiative, or your boss is delaying a decision or approval, a deadline (if one can be imposed) will usually force the issue.

Break deadlines – especially ones over long time periods – into a series of intermediate deadlines (checkpoints). For example, in the case of a report, create a deadline for completion of research, another for first draft, etc. In this way, you're constantly pushed to keep the initiative moving along.

Finally, ask someone to hold you accountable for hitting deadlines.

It can be painful, but meeting time commitments to others is a powerful behavioral incentive for everyone involved.

Allocate time for conscious incompetence

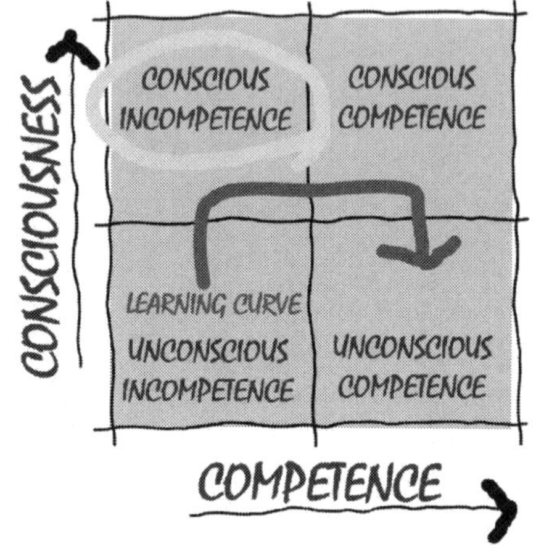

Remember the Conscious Competence Model (Chapter 3) and the challenges associated with conscious incompetence – the stage of learning where we know what to do but can't do it well?

Whenever we learn new things, such as thinking strategically in high-VUCA environments, taking on a new executive role, beginning to make strategic time, etc., we move into conscious incompetence, where quality and comfort decreases and the time it takes to do things increases.

Many executives fail to keep to their time allocations because they neglect to factor the added time it will take to learn – time they often can't anticipate until they're in the middle of the learning (something that happened to me as I wrote this book).

How much time should you allocate for conscious incompetence? Again, it's situational, but if the new activity has high volatility, unfamiliarity, complexity, and ambiguity, and you're relatively inexperienced in the tools or capabilities required for effectiveness, does allocating twice as much time as an expert feel impractical?

Under promise and over deliver

A paradox of executive life (and a shock to many new executives) is the more senior you become, the harder it is to get big, significant things done. It seems everything takes longer than it should.

There are many legitimate reasons for this. For instance, it's much harder to analyze, develop, and implement solutions to Complex and Wicked problems than Tame ones, and it takes longer to get people onside who you don't have authority over, (such as your boss, stakeholders, and colleagues) than those reporting to you. In addition, most people suffer from planning fallacy – the confidence or belief that their own project will proceed as planned, even while knowing the vast majority of similar projects have run late.[12]

As a result, especially when ideas are new or controversial, most executives vastly underestimate the time needed to move strategic initiatives successfully from ideation through acceptability to implementation.

The answer – learn to under promise and over deliver. Consult with others who have completed similar initiatives to understand issues that created delays, and propose allocations accordingly. Using the data and opinions collected, make a 'baseline allocation' that assumes problems will arise, and include a 'best-case scenario' that assumes things will work out well. Get feedback on your baseline allocation from knowledgeable peers before you commit to deadlines – challenge them to be pessimistic, and change the allocations as needed.

Finally, assume the worst. Most strategic initiatives are delivered over budget and behind time. It's overly optimistic (bordering on naive) to think your initiatives will be different unless you're sure they will be.

Allocate time in blocks to maintain long-term allocations

The key to maintaining long-term allocations is to block time in your weekly schedule dedicated to those areas of priority. Blocking time has a number of advantages. First, 15 to 30-minute segments scattered throughout a day doesn't facilitate deep thought or reflection. Second, we are more productive when we dedicate ourselves to a sequence of similar activities rather than switching back and forth between different activities. For instance, back-to-back meetings over a three-hour period are preferable to random periods of disparate activities like meeting, reading, interaction, report writing, etc. Third, creating large blocks of similar activities makes it easier to prioritize certain activities and eliminate small periods of ineffective time that often result as you transition from one activity to another.

Let's say you've allocated about 20-25% of your time to an important priority over the next four months (about 14 hours per week). To help ensure that time isn't lost to less important initiatives, block it in your calendar on a weekly basis. It may mean two hours per day during the work week and four hours spread over the weekend.

Although everyone is different, research shows certain times of day are more conducive to certain activities. For instance, strategic thinking places very different cognitive demands on us than email, interaction with others, etc. As a result, allocate strategic thinking to early mornings when you're most open to reflection and abstract or dynamic thought. Conversely, emails and other correspondence don't require that level of reflection, so block those for later in the day (the key is to block them – as much as possible avoid reacting to them unless you have no choice).

Of course, an added bonus of moving strategic thinking and other important priorities to first thing in the morning is ensuring they're done first rather than something squeezed in at the end of an exhausting day, if at all – it's a way to 'pay yourself first'.

In the following diagram, you can see one way of blocking a weekly calendar: early morning is dedicated to strategic thinking, followed by email and other correspondence, followed by business meetings and interactions with others, and ending with social commitments that may extend into the evening. To help you organize and maintain something like this, ensure your assistant is aware of your allocations and adheres to them unless they have approval to deviate (a good assistant should help hold you accountable to the commitments you've made to yourself).

Guard strategic time and do what you can to expand it. For instance, if 1:00 to 5:00 pm is time blocked for meetings, start booking meetings at the end of the day (4:30 – 5:00) and fill your schedule from back to front so that any time freed might be added to strategic thinking time or other priorities in the morning.

Avoid dead spots in your calendar. For instance, a 45-minute meeting at 2:00 pm and a 30-minute meeting at 3:00 with 15 minutes in between. Most people use those short periods between meetings for email, returning phone calls, etc., however, this means toggling between different types

	MONDAY	TUESDAY	WEDNESDAY	THURSDAY	FRIDAY
5:00					
6:00	STRATEGIC TIME	STRATEGIC TIME	STRATEGIC TIME	STRATEGIC TIME	STRATEGIC TIME
7:00		EMAIL/TO DO		EMAIL/TO DO	
8:00	GYM		GYM		GYM
9:00	EMAIL/TO DO		EMAIL/TO DO		EMAIL/TO DO
10:00	MEETING PREP	MEETINGS	MEETING PREP	MEETINGS	MEETING PREP
11:00					
12:00		CLIENT LUNCH		CLIENT LUNCH	
1:00	MEETINGS	EMAIL/TO DO	MEETINGS	EMAIL/TO DO	MEETINGS
2:00					
3:00		TRAVEL, READING & EMAIL/TO DO		TRAVEL, READING & EMAIL/TO DO	
4:00	EMAIL/TO DO		EMAIL/TO DO		EMAIL/TO DO
5:00					
6:00					
7:00	CLIENT & TEAM	FAMILY	CLIENT & TEAM	MEETING PREP	FAMILY
8:00					

NOVEMBER 18-22, 2019

of activities. To avoid this, book meetings back to back as much as possible (don't forget periodic five-minute breaks if you're using the Pomodoro technique) and block 30 to 60 minutes dedicated to correspondence, phone calls, taking action on issues that arise during meetings, etc. (of course, the more you conduct meetings by phone and teleconference, the easier it is to schedule your meetings back to back).

Use a paper calendar or time monitoring system

When it comes to allocating time, it's important to separate the forest from the trees. The former are blocks of allocated time, and the latter are the hundreds of activities and tasks that enable us to produce outcomes in those blocks of time.

I'm not familiar with all the time-management apps on the market, so some may do a good job of providing a global view of your schedule - they're getting better every day but I haven't found one that works for me. However, most executives I work with find time allocations and timelines done on paper or a whiteboard give them a fuller, overall perspective for how they'll block their calendars to achieve priorities over long time periods, i.e. a month, quarter, year and/or longer.

Conclusion

Allocating strategic time is all about setting priorities. It's carving out future time for the big things you're trying to accomplish in your life and work. Without allocating strategic time, executives risk 'frittering themselves away operating.' Allocating starts with getting clear about why strategic time is so important to you personally, envisioning a desirable future state, and having lots of alternate ways of blocking the time needed to get you there.

Topics we covered in Chapter 6 – Allocate strategic time – spot the high ground.

Topic	Page
• Introduction	77
• Allocate strategic time – guiding principles	79
• How do you see yourself?	79
• Why do you want to make strategic time?	80
• Envision a desired future state	82
• Executive teams need shared priorities	83
• Be clear about what you won't do	84
• Write priorities/time allocations down	84
• Remind yourself as often as possible	85
• How much strategic time do you need to allocate?	86
• Allocate more 'high importance/low urgency' time	87
• Allocate time based on time span	88
• Allocate time based on inside/outside focus	90
• Pomodoro technique – conserving energy	91
• Allocate time based on key functions	92
• Maintain control of your top priorities	94
• Always have an active, significant strategic priority	94
• Always work to a deadline	95
• Allocate time for conscious incompetence	96
• Under promise and over deliver	96
• Allocate time in blocks to maintain long-term allocations	97
• Use a paper calendar or time monitoring system	99
• Conclusion	100

7

MONITOR STRATEGIC TIME – GET THE LAY OF THE LAND

'What gets measured gets managed.' – Peter Drucker

Introduction

THERE'S AN OLD saying, 'Don't tell me your priorities, show me your calendar.'

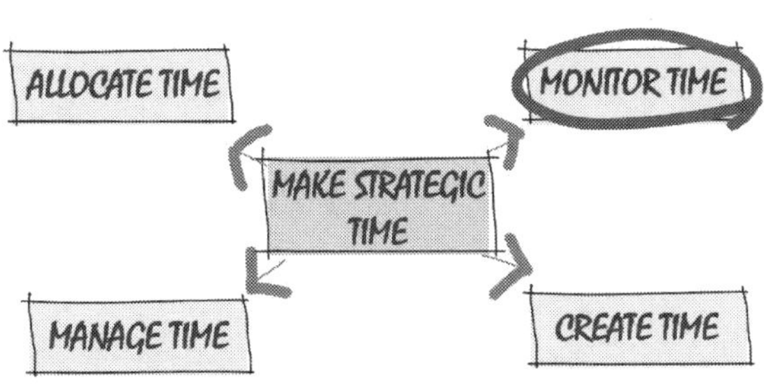

Many people have similar priorities, for example, maintain a healthy weight, make strategic time, etc. But it's usually only those who consistently deploy the tools and techniques needed to turn intentions into actions and behavior that achieve their goals. After all, talk is cheap.

Every executive knows the wisdom of Peter Drucker's maxim, 'What gets measured gets managed,' but how often do you systematically measure and monitor how your time is being used? Drucker says, 'One cannot even think of managing one's time unless one first knows where it goes.'[1] Without measurement and monitoring, most time allocations – like most other commitments we make to ourselves – just become empty promises.

Over 90% of executives regularly fail to make the strategic time they feel their role demands. At the risk of offending, that's a dismal record in a key area of executive effectiveness.

Monitoring performance is the basis of change and improvement because it tells you whether you're maintaining your time allocations and suggests what must be changed to get back on track. Without it, you're flying blind.

Monitor strategic time – guiding principles

Before looking at time-monitoring strategies and tactics, let's outline a few principles to help guide us.

- Keep the process simple – the harder it is to monitor your time, the less likely you'll make the time and energy to do it; and

- Standardize – identify three to four key metrics (key performance indicators) that relate back to your time allocations and review them regularly.

Conduct a calendar/schedule audit

Almost every executive knows where they want their time to go – they have an intuitive sense they need to get out of the weeds and put their time and focus on highest-level problems.

However, when executives compare where time should be going against where it's actually going, they usually see a large gap – even when they're clear about how they want to allocate their time.

I recently asked each member of a senior executive team, 'In order to have maximum impact on the organization and your career, what four or five areas must receive most of your time?' Their responses indicated that they knew exactly where their primary focus should be – each laid out four or five broad areas of strategic importance to the organization and/or highest-level problems, for example, 30% of time should be in one place, 20% of time in another, etc. However, when they used their electronic calendars to review the previous three weeks, they weren't even close.

This is a very common situation. Regularly conducting a simple calendar or schedule audit should be a standard procedure for every executive - something they do at least every three months. Your audit should start with your time allocations. If you haven't already created time allocations, refer to Chapter 6.

Now review your calendar and assign activities, i.e. meetings, report writing, interactions with others, etc., to the appropriate time allocation. For instance, a CFO I worked with had determined she wanted to allocate 30% of her time to overseeing the M&A process and 20% to upgrading the finance function. As she reviewed her calendar, she assigned activities to the appropriate allocations. These two areas were relatively distinct so it was easy to determine where activities should be allocated, however, when an activity covered both topics, she allocated the time for that specific activity to the area that benefited most. (Incidentally, the calendar audit revealed she was spending hardly any time in each area.)

Where there's a gap between your time allocations and your activities, consider the principal cause(s) for the discrepancy. Are the original allocations unreasonable? If yes, make appropriate adjustments. Is the discrepancy a short-term one caused by unforeseen circumstances? If yes, create a deadline for when you want things back on track.

A word of caution – resist the temptation to adjust original time allocations. Even though your time allocations may be aspirational, there's a good reason you made them in the first place, so fight for them.

If your schedule is clearly off track with your time allocations, make adjustments ASAP – Chapter 8 contains many ideas for taking action. In my experience, without regularly conducting calendar audits, it's virtually impossible to make and maintain strategic time.

Track your time daily or weekly

I've been a 'time-based professional' (consultant) for over 30 years, and when the term 'time based' is used to refer to your occupation, it's natural to assume you're an expert at allocating and monitoring time usage. After all, in consulting, time is the basis for revenue projections, tracking progress towards those projections, planning and allocating staff on projects, preparing billings, etc., so you'd expect all consultants to be good at it.

However, you'd be wrong. Even with access to very sophisticated time-tracking systems, most time-based professionals find monitoring time one of their least desirable and successful activities.

If you want proof, a 2015 survey of 500 professionals at a services automation consulting firm estimated that each consultant lost $50,000 per year in revenue due to insufficient time tracking of emails with clients and others. (2) In the face of considerable resistance from their people, accounting firm KPMG threatened their UK employees with a 100-pound fine if they failed to submit weekly time records on time. (3)

Why am I telling you this? Because the advice I'm about to provide is not easy to implement – if you want an accurate sense for where your time is going, you should reconcile it (record it, code it) against your time allocations at least once per day (ideally twice a day). For instance, record the time you spend in the morning, at noon, and the time spent in the afternoon, at the end of the day.

The reason for this is simple. The longer you wait to record your time, the lower the accuracy. For instance, some studies show that waiting one or two days can cut accuracy significantly. (4) In other words, if you're not going to track your time daily, it's probably not worth doing it all.

There are a number of promising, time-tracking software apps in the market, for example, RescueTime, BQE Core, Time Doctor, etc. that track your time automatically. Many executives I speak with don't use them because they worry about overcomplicating things or the learning curve they associate (rightly or wrongly) with learning new technologies is too steep. Having said that, they're definitely worth a try.

A technique available to anyone with a computer is to keep a simple Excel spreadsheet open with columns that track their time against their allocations. For instance, I currently allocate my time to three broad areas: Creative (55% of my time), Client Work (30% of my time), and Other (15% of my time). You may recognize this allocation – it's modeled after the one that the author Jim Collins uses, referred to in Chapter 6.

Creative includes three sub-allocations – Research (10% of my time), Marketing (10% of my time), and Development (35% of my time). Client Work time includes all preparation and delivery I undertake on behalf of clients, subdivided by client name. Other is anything that doesn't fit into the first two allocations.

I set a recurring Outlook reminder for noon and 5:00 p.m. each day and pause whatever I'm doing to enter my time (if I miss an entry, I catch up at the next scheduled entry time). Accuracy is high (which it certainly needs to be for clients).

It's easy to roll this information up into a weekly, monthly, or quarterly snapshot. For instance, over the past month, my Creative time is running over budget (over 60% compared to my targeted 55%), while Client Work and Other are slightly under budget. I'm OK with this, although Marketing (part of my Creative work) dipped more than it should, so I've made an adjustment.

This simple approach offers multiple benefits. It's easy and quick – I spend about a minute a day tracking time. I can see where I've deviated from my allocations at a glance and can adjust accordingly. I've also estimated how many hours I think a specific key project should take and can quickly compare where I currently stand against that projection.

Many find regularly monitoring their time gives them a better appreciation for the importance of time to their effectiveness. For instance, if you've allocated 30% of your time this month to a specific priority and find by mid-month you're tracking well behind, it's motivation to strongly resist further distractions.

Leading versus lagging indicators

Lagging indicators measure outcomes. For instance, weighing myself at the end of a week is an example of a lagging indicator. It tells me my excessive eating and lack of exercise over the past week has resulted in weight gain. Unfortunately there's nothing I can do to fix last week.

Leading indicators measure input and predict outcome. If losing weight is a goal for the next two weeks, I must allocate time and attention to reducing my food intake and increasing exercise. Eating and exercise are leading indicators – by tracking them I can predict weight gain if I increase the former while reducing the latter.

As it relates to making strategic time, calendar and schedule audits are examples of lagging indicators. Examples of leading indicators are: established priorities that focus on highest-level problems, allocations that designate an appropriate amount of time for strategic thinking and daily reminders for tracking time. With these leading indicators firmly in place, your chances of making and maintaining strategic time are increased.

How are we doing right now – are we at the right level?

Have you ever been in an executive team meeting and wondered how and why the group's gotten focused on an irrelevant topic or agenda item, going down a rabbit hole and focusing on issues of little consequence?

If you have, you know it's easy for executive teams to get sucked into the weeds – even when they know they're supposed to focus on Wicked problems, they're continuously pulled into lower level ones. We talked about how groups or teams get stuck in the weeds in Chapter 4, but didn't talk about what to do when it happens or how to avoid it altogether.

For starters, the primary responsibility for keeping a team properly focused falls to the leader or chairperson. To help with that, every two to three months (at least) they should ask themselves, 'How are we doing right now?'

This question is intentionally high level. Just as a doctor's check-up focuses on vital signs like blood pressure, weight, etc., because they reveal the potential for underlying issues, the leader should focus on strategic vital signs. Those specific signs will vary from leader to leader, but a few examples I've seen include: is the full senior team aligned on the organization's direction – do they have a shared 'picture' of the organization in three to five years (or some other date in the future)? Given what the senior team is trying to accomplish in the next few years, is it focused at the right level of problem difficulty? What's the biggest strategic challenge facing the organization that we're not talking about? Are key stakeholders fully onside? Is trust between our key executives as high as it needs to be? Given our long-term goals, is the operating model and/or culture right?

Of course, if the answers to these questions (and/or other similar ones) are unsatisfactory, they represent good opportunities for full executive team discussion – at least as valuable as 'Did we hit last month's numbers?'

These simple questions may seem obvious, but I've watched many teams go about their business even when everyone knows the vital signs are bad. If the leader isn't regularly asking, 'How are we doing right now?', others should.

Is this working for me?

Just as the previous section advocated that groups and teams regularly monitor effectiveness, this section proposes individuals regularly do the same for themselves.

I've met very few executives who don't want to be as good at their job as they can be; the best possible version of themselves. Then they're dragged into the weeds, drowning in issues and behaviors that stifle those good intentions.

We've talked before about how it's easy to get so tied up in actions and reactions on the treadmill of life that we forget to make sure our days are leading to important goals like fulfillment, effectiveness, happiness, career or organizational success, etc. So periodically, for example once per quarter or semi-annually (at least), look at your calendar and ask, 'Is this working for me?'

When your answer is a resounding 'no' (or even 'I don't think so') it's time to revisit what you're doing against what you're trying to achieve, to remind yourself why your goals are so important to you and recommit to what you're going to say yes and no to.

Many people need to reach the point of peak frustration before they ask 'Is this working for me?' In my view, this can lead to big, life-altering decisions more reflective of frustration than rational analysis. Instead, scheduling a time to reflect enables you to course correct before things get too far off the rails.

Regularly assess the effectiveness of meetings

Meetings are a critical management tool, and the typical executive spends over 50% of their time in meetings. In a survey conducted on behalf of Harvard Business Review, 71% of respondents said that meetings are unproductive and inefficient, and 64% said they come at the expense of time for strategic thinking.[(5)] Maybe that's why dysfunctional meeting behaviors are associated with lower levels of market share, innovation and employment stability.[(5)]

As a result, making meetings as effective as possible represents a great opportunity to add value to the organization and make productive strategic time. Yet, I've seen many executives regularly attend the same dysfunctional meetings over and over without addressing the issues that make them that way. For instance, griping, complaining and blaming are readily noticeable, and directly linked to low team effectiveness[(6)] yet are often allowed to persist from meeting to meeting.

To avoid dysfunctional meeting behavior, I recommend the meeting chair – individually or in concert with meeting participants – assess the quality of meetings on a regular basis to identify issues and resolve them as soon as possible. One simple idea - immediately following every second or third meeting – when memories of the meeting are fresh – the chair takes five minutes to reflect on one or two things that can be improved. This includes pre-meeting preparation and/or post-meeting follow-up. At the start of the next meeting, inform the group about new practices, and put them into effect.

Alternatively, during the last five minutes of a meeting, periodically ask participants 'What's one thing we can do to make these meetings more productive?' Each participant usually has a thought, and if two to three bring the same idea forward, it's likely a source of broad dissatisfaction. If honesty within the group is high, collect responses on a flip chart or white board. Alternatively, ask people to send their suggestions by email after the meeting. Again, at the next meeting, implement the new practice.

If you don't think the meeting's going well, don't wait until it's over to make improvements. Instead ask 'How well is this meeting working right now?' If participants agree that it's not going well, ask, 'What's one thing we can do right now to get back on track?' Having participants involved in the monitoring process reminds them that everyone bears responsibility for meeting effectiveness and expands the number of improvement ideas.

An effective technique that's rarely used is to ask a participant to step out of the group (five to 10 feet if possible) and observe the meeting from afar as it progresses. It's harder to see what's happening in a group when you're part of it, observing from outside the group provides objectivity. Ideally, the person observes for about 10 minutes, reports on their observations as they rejoin the meeting, and the group adjusts behaviors accordingly.

Finally, I think there's great value in receiving the objective, expert opinion of a qualified executive team coach. To get the most out of this option, ensure they have experience working with executive teams facing levels of problem difficulty similar to the ones your team is facing and they evaluate your team while it's working on solving highest-level problems.

I've seen executive teams utilize two or more of these techniques in combination to radically reduce time-wasting practices and quickly elevate the effectiveness of their meetings.

Of course, it's also a great idea to monitor meeting effectiveness with 'hard' metrics. For instance, use a short evaluation form to track things like attendance, whether meetings start and end on time, meeting participation (how often or little did individuals speak), number of action items opened and closed, and number of decisions made. Over time, trends may emerge that demand attention, and hard data helps make the case for change.

For instance, I use a powerful 'hard' measurement tool to expose flaws in the way teams manage dialogue. It incorporates the Four Player Model developed by David Kantor[7] who proposes effective dialogue requires a mixture of four different roles or positions: Moving, Opposing, Standing-By, and Following (his book and the internet have information on how to deploy this very helpful model).

When a group or team is struggling with dialogue, I ask them to engage in a problem-solving discussion as they normally would and track the number of roles/positions used. It's not unusual to see issues that prevent good dialogue and provide insights that enable the team to immediately take corrective action.

Conclusion

When it comes to strategic time, the old maxim, 'What gets measured gets managed' has never been truer. Monitoring time means tracking how your time's being used as consistently, accurately, and as simply as possible, and then comparing it to the time allocations (promises) you've made and closing inevitable gaps as quickly as possible. For most people, monitoring isn't much fun – without it, you're not going to make strategic time.

Topics we covered in Chapter 7 – Monitor strategic time – get the lay of the land.

Topic	Page
• Introduction	103
• Monitor strategic time – guiding principles	104
• Conduct a calendar/schedule audit	104
• Track your time daily or weekly	106
• Leading versus lagging indicators	107
• How are we doing right now – are we at the right level?	108
• Is this working for me?	109
• Regularly assess the effectiveness of meetings	110
• Conclusion	112

CREATE STRATEGIC TIME – PULL WEEDS

'I will have to remember, I am here today to cross the swamp, not to fight all the alligators.' — From The Art of Possibility by Rosamund and Benjamin Zadler.

Introduction

BECAUSE THE TYPICAL executive has the 119 waking hours of their week jammed with intense activity, the ability to make strategic time by working longer and harder is questionable.

Sure, you can sleep less and reduce time spent on family, friends, personal interests, etc., for a short to moderate duration, but eventually there's a big price to pay, and it doesn't guarantee the time you make will be strategic time. At some point, it's time for something more creative.

Creation is the process of bringing something to life that hasn't previously existed. There are four simple strategies available to every executive for creating strategic time.

First, review your calendar and take a knife to as many 'urgent but not important' tasks immediately. If you can't dump or delegate it today, take steps to drop it or stop it ASAP.

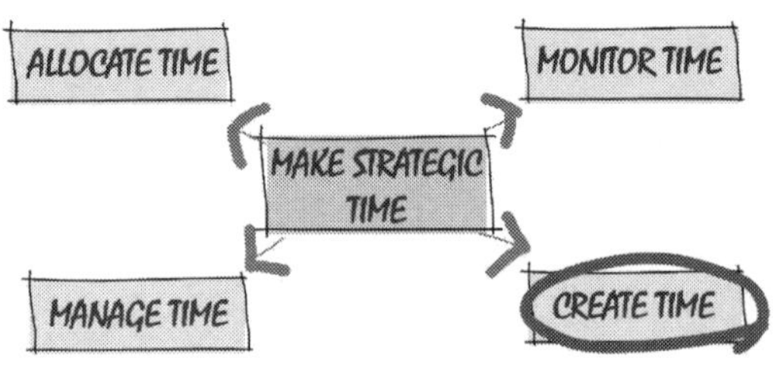

Second, remember the best way to drop or stop something is to not start it in the first place – saying no to something gives you an opportunity to say yes to something more meaningful.

STRATEGIES FOR CREATING TIME

1. DROP IT/STOP IT
2. JUST SAY NO
3. NEGOTIATE
4. REDESIGN

Third, when you can't say no (important stakeholders, clients, situations, etc. demand your time) do your best to negotiate the scope of your commitment, for example, quick huddles instead of formal meetings, conference calls instead of face-to-face meetings, regularly negotiating shorter meetings, etc.

Finally, redesign inefficient processes that kill productivity, such as email, voicemail, meetings, reporting, and other productivity-killing practices. Increased productivity is recaptured time.

The unintended consequences of work make it difficult for executives to make strategic time, however, many overwhelmed executives quickly free two to six hours per week (or more) if all four strategies are regularly applied.

Create strategic time – guiding principles

Before diving into time-creating tactics, let's outline a few principles to help guide us:

- Perfection is the enemy of good – you don't have to solve every time challenge to derive significant benefit. Creating three hours of strategic time is better than none at all;

- Look for leverage – find a tactic that works well and apply it everywhere, or address those situations that represent your biggest time losses first; and

- Always be creating – adopt the mindset that strategic time is your most critical resource (because it is) so you're always applying one or more time-creating strategies.

Use to-do lists

Almost everyone is so familiar with to-do lists (and possibly fed up with them) that I'm a bit embarrassed to list them as a way of creating time. However, well known does not always mean well used.

A principal benefit of a to-do list is that you don't have to use valuable cognitive power to keep track of things – the list does it for you so you can focus on higher-level issues – and fewer tasks drop through the cracks.

I recommend keeping two lists – one for tasks requiring completion over the next month (broken down by week) and one for the upcoming week (broken down by day). Review your weekly list at the end of each day (or some other time that's convenient), cross off completed tasks, (always a wonderful feeling) carry over uncompleted tasks, and review the next day's list.

As a rule of thumb, don't exceed 10 tasks per day or you'll find yourself carrying things over to the next day (a terrible feeling). As much as possible, block a time during your day for task completion – preferably mid-morning or later. During your day, if something comes up, make every effort to move it to an upcoming day rather than adding it on today's list – it will likely just mean something you've scheduled to do today will get pushed into another day.

Stick to one method of list keeping so all lists are kept in one place. For years, I used a small black book to track my to-do lists, but have recently switched to a free app called Todoist which I find very user friendly (the wonderful Wunderlist app has been closed down). The learning curve is very short, you can easily share tasks with others (supports delegation), schedule notifications, carry over uncompleted tasks, prioritize tasks, and monitor the number of tasks for a given day. It also automatically breaks your full task list into any number of sub-lists, such as daily and weekly tasks and actions related to specific projects or initiatives, etc. There are other apps on the market, and a free one is a great place to start experimenting with an electronic to-do list. In the short time I've used one, I feel it's increased my efficiency a great deal.

Go digital as soon as possible

I still see far too many executives who resist or struggle with new digital time management and communication tools. Some still have their assistant print emails for their review and response. It's the equivalent of having ice delivered to your house instead of buying a fridge that makes it automatically.

I understand the reticence. Time-constrained people don't feel they've got the time needed to learn something new, and just when the latest technology's been mastered, something better hits the market. However, most new applications are so intuitive that they flatten the learning curve dramatically, and it's surprisingly easy to transfer skills used in one application to another. The best part – they really do reduce the time and effort associated with many tasks.

To help me make more strategic time, I've taken to a number of new digital aids and am pleasantly surprised at how they've increased my productivity. How to get started? I used to read material to build my understanding of a new app, but now I just dive in and learn as I go, consulting other users when I'm stumped.

A worst-case scenario – you've encouraged the team you lead to use electronic collaborative and teaming tools (more on them later), but you stick with paper and email. Now they're forced to use two systems, one for communicating with one another and one for keeping you in the loop – you're eating up your own precious time, and now you're doing the same to them.

Delegation

There's an old expression, 'If you want something done right, do it yourself.' It's not true, but it persists.

Delegation is the act of assigning a responsibility you hold to someone else. As a general rule, I recommend executives adopt the mindset to delegate everything (they possibly can) that does not have a material impact on the highest-level problems and priorities they've allocated their time to.

As we know, that's easier said than done, particularly when an executive's high standards or even higher diligence [(1)] create a reluctance to delegate. In addition, many feel that completing a lower-level task takes less time than assigning it to others, especially when it necessitates training and performance oversight; it's more productive to just do it themselves. Finally, many are simply not as good at delegation and managing performance as they could be.[(2)]

However, I challenge you to look at your 'to-do' list for the day or week, and really ask yourself whether it's simply habit (possibly some laziness or inertia) that has you holding on to tasks others should and could do. Besides, if you don't start delegating, you're never going to learn how to do it well. The basics of good delegation are very easy to learn, and assigning responsibilities with minimal risk to direct reports (or others) with a proven track record of high conscientiousness and competence is a great place to start.

Here are three delegation tips my clients find particularly helpful (there are many others).[(3)] First, delegate responsibilities rather than tasks – make others responsible for sorting out the tasks and ensuring they deliver intended outcomes. Second, clarify expectations carefully and ask those responsible to report their understanding back to you so you can gauge whether they've internalized things correctly. Finally, agree on reporting, i.e. fix a date and time for a quick check-in (30–60 seconds) to gauge progress and provide feedback and support if needed.

I bet there are responsibilities you can assign to others today. If you don't get good at delegation, your opportunities for making strategic time will dwindle fast.

Dictation

A simple and quick redesign to non-verbal communication can create strategic time.

If you type well, you've got a leg up in today's world because the majority of non-verbal communication involves typing – Instagram, Facebook, Twitter, emails, reports, PowerPoint slides, blogs, notes to oneself, etc.

However, typing well might discourage you from using dictation even though it's free, (it's included in many computer applications) easy to download, accurate, simple to use, (after a short learning curve) and a significant time saver – even a good typist can speak five to eight times faster than they can type (the more formal the message the lower the speed). Dictation can be used very effectively for emails, texts, notes to files, etc.

Many executives routinely deal with over 200 emails a day, eating up five to six hours of time per week (more on getting better control of email later). If dictation saves you 25% of that, you've created a little over an hour of additional strategic time per week without changing anything else - it's why I now dictate 80% of my emails and texts.

Better reading habits

Because executives spend so much time reading work-related books, reports, PowerPoint decks, etc., there are a number of time-saving ideas that will enable you take in more information in less time.

First, be very particular about what you read. Not reading something at all is a great time saver. To help with this, I've stopped reading magazines and periodicals unless I'm conducting research and can be very specific about what I'm looking for. I've also started using Twitter to push subjects from acknowledged experts on topics directly related to my work. In addition, I've become very wary of the full entertainment system we all carry everywhere we go – our phones – and the accumulated waste that quick five to 10-minute check-ins to news and social media sites can have over the course of a day. According to RescueTime, (an app that measures phone usage) the average person spends just over three hours per day reading on their phones – most of it completely unrelated to strategic priorities.

Second, batch your reading. I usually have a colleague photocopy articles I want to read or drop links into an electronic file (Evernote and OneNote are two examples) and read them all together (usually while flying or at a time during my week I've specifically allocated to reading). I also have a rule – no sports or news consumption during the workday (which I'm not always successful enforcing).

Third, read instead of watching videos, television, etc. For instance, TED talks are entertaining, but their information can be consumed three to four times faster by reading a transcript or article on the subject. If you absolutely must watch a video or listen to a podcast, use the 10–15 second advance button to speed-watch/listen (you can often accelerate the rate of speech by 1.5 times as well).

Fourth, speed-read. When trying to comprehend something deeply, most of us read 200–400 words per minute. In a relatively short period of time, most can learn to speed-read 400–700 words per minute (or faster). That's this whole book between 90-150 minutes while maintaining moderate comprehension and spotting key information you may want to revisit.

I took a one-hour speed-reading course when I started my MBA, and despite a relatively steep learning curve (I love words and I resisted skimming them so quickly) I soon devoured stacks of information while retaining most of the critical stuff. Speed-reading basics are found on many websites, and they're easy to learn and apply. Build your technique and confidence with material of lesser importance, and gradually expand to most or all your business reading.

Over time, if a combination of these techniques doesn't save at least one to two hours a week, I'd be surprised.

The primary purpose of team meetings – enable better decisions

Meetings can have four primary purposes:

- Information sharing – the sharing of data between different people and parts of the organization;
- Consultation – tapping into the expertise of an individual to help resolve a problem or situation;
- Coordination – the process of organizing people or groups of people so they work more effectively together; and
- Decision-making – the act or process of making a decision.

As much as possible, the primary purpose of executive meetings should be dialogue that leads to better decision-making – even when the actual decision isn't made during the meeting – because little happens until decisions are made. The road to good decision-making often breaks down before the meeting starts. For instance, over 90% of executives say their company doesn't have a rigorous process for ensuring the agenda is focusing the team on the organization's most significant issues.[4]

When an executive wants to make a decision on their own or with input from others, meetings are a primary way for them to compare and contrast differing views, evaluate the merit of different positions, and co-create solutions. When the meeting leader decides to make a decision collectively, meetings are the best forum for collaborative decision-making.

Ensure valuable meeting time is spent on topics relevant to all participants. Most information sharing, i.e. research, updates, status reports, etc., is best conducted as meeting pre-work so participants have time to effectively read, reflect, and analyze in preparation for meeting dialogue. Most information sharing, consultation, and coordination is conducted more effectively by email or telephone outside the meeting between those with a 'need to know'. The same goes for the review of actions or accountabilities flowing from a meeting.

Jeff Bezos, CEO of Amazon, says, 'as a senior executive, you get paid to make a small number of high quality decisions. If I make three good decisions a day, that's enough'. As much as possible, when your executive team is meeting, use that time for deciding something.

Put a value on time

If I approach you and suggest I'll give you a $20 bill in exchange for a $100 bill, you'll look at me like I need my head examined (unfortunately). However, most executives earn a lot more than $100 dollars an hour, but gladly spend an hour on something that delivers $20 of value. It's the same bad deal.

The executive compensation you receive is in return for a commensurate level of value. When you're in the weeds, you're cheating yourself and the organization. There are going to be times you deliver relatively low value because no one can put 100% of their time towards key priorities. However, that time should be kept to a minimum and offset with very high-value time as much as possible.

Review your schedule for the upcoming week. Are most activities delivering the value your compensation assumes? If not, can you dump most of the low-value time? This impetus to focus on high-value activities includes the creation of meeting agendas. For instance, consider the 'value-at-stake' of an agenda item, i.e. its impact on the long-term value to the organization, before adding it to an executive agenda.[(4)]

I once worked for someone who kept a $100 bill in a small acrylic case on the side of his desk. He made a lot more than that per hour but kept it there to remind himself how valuable time is – it prompted him to say no to low-value requests and stay out of the weeds.

Reduce the number of people in meetings

The saying, 'Too many chefs spoil the broth' is as relevant to meetings as kitchens. Generally, the more people attending a meeting, the less efficient and productive it becomes because everything takes more time. More people increases time needed for conversation, the likelihood of starting and running late, and the time needed for reaching consensus, etc.

In many meetings, 20% of participants tend to create 80% of the value because individual participants make unequal contributions. For instance, some don't have requisite knowledge, struggle to keep up or don't speak, etc. Very often, some participants would be better deployed elsewhere so their participation doesn't take time from more crucial participants.

Most meetings have too many participants because invitation lists aren't vetted closely and people have reasons to attend other than a valued contribution to the meeting. For instance, many meetings confer power through association with powerful attendees, knowledge imparted, and participation in key decisions. Some attend meetings to build relationships and their title provides access even when they're not making a valuable contribution.

However, these aren't sound criteria for participation in meetings. Instead, base participation on an attendee's ability to provide information necessary to the meeting, arrive adequately prepared to make a meaningful contribution, and play a key role in the decision-making process. This implies they must have approval rights, decision rights, and/or a key role or responsibility in implementation.

This issue of attendance is doubly important as meeting formality increases. There are essentially six different ways people tackle problems, ranging from working alone to working in a standing team.

As the frequency and difficulty of problems increase, so does the formality of the groups solving them. For instance, when problem difficulty and problem frequency are low, the most productive way to proceed is 'phone a friend' – just two people having a quick chat.

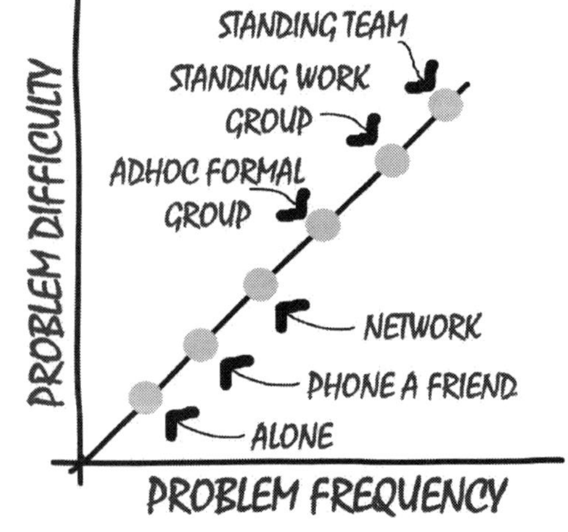

However, members of standing workgroups and teams meet regularly over time because the high frequency of very difficult problems demand regular attention – all members attend almost every meeting. As a result, when leaders compose their teams, they must carefully consider the ability of members to solve current and future problems, keeping the number of participants to its optimum size.

How many people are ideal for standing team meetings? It depends on group purpose and the level of VUCA or problem difficulty. For teams primarily focused on information sharing, consultation and coordination, 11–12 people are manageable, especially with the effective use of sub-committees.

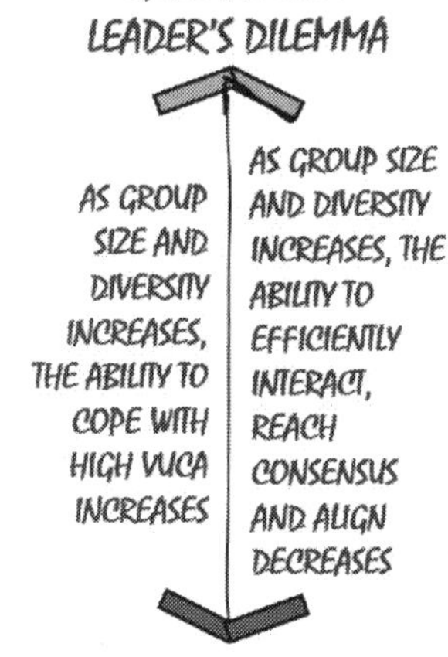

For decision-making groups in high-VUCA environments, the ideal composition appears to be between six and eight people (including the chair). Fewer than six people may dilute the knowledge and diversity needed for effective strategic thinking, and greater than eight may make interaction, consensus, and alignment difficult to achieve.

However, as VUCA and problem difficulty drops, so does ideal team size – when it's low, five to six people are ideal (always keep in mind the Rule of Seven – every meeting participant over seven makes it 10% harder to make a decision).[4]

Because most executives are facing rising VUCA, team size is elevating along with the amount of time spent in meetings. As a result, I recommend the chair review team composition and invitation lists on a regular basis (once per quarter) because both significantly affect problem-solving effectiveness, productivity, and the use of time.

At the same time, regularly hold meeting participants to very high expectations or expect the productive use of strategic time to plummet. The chair should immediately make their criteria or expectations for meeting participation clear. Once expectations are clear, review them periodically with the team or individuals who are falling below standard, and hold them accountable for improved behavior. In addition, make it known that participation in meetings is not automatic – the team leader reserves the right to expand or contract the group as things evolve. It's a great way to increase commitment to the meetings, and gives participants the freedom to drop meetings when they're no longer required to attend.

Finally, when the purpose of the meetings shifts, examine whether changes in the number and type of participants should follow. Always try to get by with as few as possible – or disband the group altogether if it makes sense so that participant time can be deployed in more productive ways.

When it comes to strategic thinking and tackling highest-level problems, meetings are both essential and the greatest cause of mismanaged and unproductive executive time. As a result, my simple recommendation to 'create strategic time by reducing the number of people in meetings' is a lot more complicated than it sounds, because it inevitably impacts problem-solving capability and issues like prestige, power, authority, and control.

That's why it deserves a lot more attention than it typically gets.

Clarify and agree on the decision-making process

A few years ago, I worked with a senior leader and his team to help resolve their struggle with a collaborative decision. The leader wanted to create a significant new role that would add a level of reporting between him and his senior team. To facilitate buy-in, he wanted the decision to be 'collaborative' – everyone would have a vote and the majority would rule.

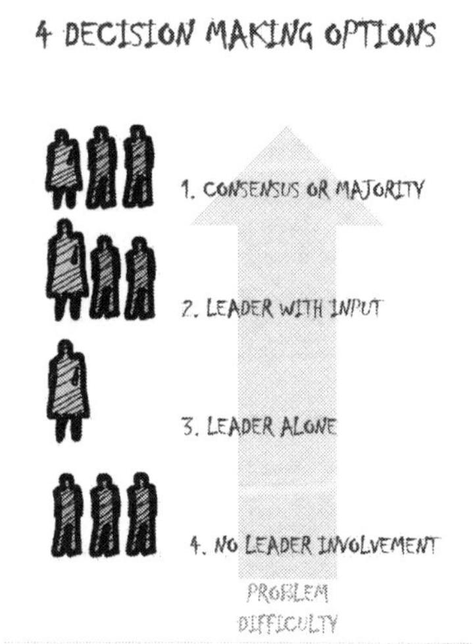

Unfortunately, two people on the team wanted the role for themselves and collected enough support to render every collaborative vote a tie. When I arrived, the situation was ongoing for four months, the team was split, wasting time in dialogue that always came back to the same place, and the leader was unable to fill the role he needed.

I began by clarifying that there are four ways to make decisions, and the leader decides which will be used for a particular decision – the method for decision-making driven by the level of difficulty posed by the problem.

First, the team makes the decision collaboratively, usually in the form of a vote (including the leader), and the decision is made by one of the following: consensus (everyone agrees to move forward with the decision without a vote), unanimity (everyone's in agreement as determined by a vote), or majority (the majority of votes wins the day). Making decisions collaboratively often takes the most time for everyone involved but can be advantageous, especially for Complex and Wicked problems.

Second, the leader makes the decision themselves with input from others – this is the next fastest way to decide because the leader can gauge how much consultation they want or need based on the situation.

Third, the leader makes the decision themselves without any input – the fastest way for leaders to make decisions because it requires little or no time for consultation.

Finally, the leader can have the group decide without their involvement. This method is ideal for Tame problems and uses the least amount of the leader's time. When the decision is turned over to the group, the leader can determine the decision-making process to be used or appoint a 'leader' for the group and let them decide.

Ideally, the leader always determines the method they'll use for deciding before dialogue on the subject begins. However, in my example above, the method chosen wasn't working and much time had been wasted with lobbying and rancorous, time-wasting debate that had delayed an important decision. I reminded the leader he has the authority to determine the decision-making method 'at any time', and given four clear choices on how to make the decision, the leader decided to make it on his own with input.

He worried this change in 'midstream' might increase disagreement with the decision and make people less likely to fully accept it – a legitimate concern. I explained that while it's great for team members to agree with a decision, it's OK for them to disagree as long as they 'align' to it.

Alignment is committing to go along with a decision whether you agree with it or not. Without alignment, anyone could hold up decisions simply by not agreeing (a common occurrence when organizational resources are at stake). As a result, no matter how leaders make a decision, they must count (insist) on every group or team member aligning whether they agree with it or not. Otherwise, significant time is wasted as people negotiate for change or go their own way, making implementation a nightmare.

I recommend that executives adopt the four decision-making processes and concept of alignment outlined above. They give dialogue greater focus, increase meeting effectiveness, remove confusion over roles, clarify the information needed for decision-making, contribute to greater alignment, and save precious strategic time.

In addition, have your direct reports understand and incorporate these two concepts into all of their meetings with the expectation that they'll have those that report to them do the same.

Keep people focused on the 'task at hand'

Years ago, my work made it necessary for me to attend meetings with our local city council. Every motion spawned multiple contributions from every councillor, most unrelated to the topic at hand – it was the gold standard for time wasting, but hardly unique to city councils.

Using speeches or stories to avoid the topic at hand, grandstand or otherwise attract attention, overexplain and settle scores is subtly pervasive. Three common tactics to watch: describing 'how things used to be done around here', restating a problem without insight or solution, or blaming a problem on forces outside the group's control.

Over 90% of meeting participants admit to daydreaming and missing parts of meetings, and over 70% say they bring other work to the meeting. [(5)] No wonder 65–75% of executive team meetings are information sharing sessions that don't end in decision [(4)] and 37% of meetings are said to be adding no value to the organization. [(5)]

A time-honored way to focus attention on decisions is Robert's Rules of Order (Robert's Rules). Originally published by US army officer Henry Martin Roberts in 1876, Robert's Rules were adapted from those used by the US Congress and amended to suit non-legislative societies.

Because most executive teams avoid Robert's Rules, a handy decision-making device – the 'motion' – is often lost. A motion is essentially a proposed decision, for instance, once recognized by the chair, a speaker says, 'I move we do X.' If the motion is seconded, a discussion ensues focused on the motion.

By putting the proposed decision up front, everyone's clear on what the discussion is for the sake of – ensuring information has a clear focus as it's leading to a binding decision. Motions essentially guide discussion towards decisions.

You don't need Robert's Rules to apply the principles of motions. Instead, before a discussion starts, ensure the topic is 'owned' by someone responsible for bringing it to the meeting. The owner starts discussion by introducing the topic (preferably in writing on flipchart or paper to reduce misinterpretation) along with the decision they want the group to make. This ensures discussion is linked to a proposed decision or action and the group knows what's being considered (and why). Ideally, the main points of the ensuing discussion are tracked – again, flipchart is preferred so everyone can see what's been discussed – and the final decision is written out so there's no confusion about what's been decided (it subsequently forms part of the minutes). An added bonus of this process is when the group is OK with the proposed decision as initially presented, they can approve it without wasting time on further discussion.

You might be surprised at how this very simple tactic saves time and improves decision-making. Less discussion, more decisions.

Always have a qualified meeting chairperson

A meeting chairperson's (chair's) responsibility is to ensure the time allotted for a meeting produces desired outcomes.

This includes managing the process for collecting potential agenda items, deciding on what makes the cut/what doesn't, and ensuring meeting logistics are appropriate to the meeting's purpose – enough time set aside, physical setting and tools or equipment are appropriate, etc. They also determine meeting conduct, including pre-work, post-meeting follow-up, the quality of dialogue during the meeting – processes for making decisions, alignment, etc.

The effectiveness of the chair might be the difference between one hour of meeting time resulting in a sound decision versus eight one-hour meetings with no decision. Despite this, I often see executive meetings where the leader doesn't chair the meeting effectively – they don't know how or neglect to fill the role – and no one else steps up. Essentially, no one's really in charge of the meeting.

Clearly, leaders need to learn to chair meetings as well as possible and if they don't, ensure that every meeting is chaired by the team member most skilled in the role. In fact, having someone other than the group leader chair a meeting gives them a chance to develop meeting leadership skills in others and enables the leader to focus on content while the meeting runs well.

Relinquishing the chair does not mean relinquishing decision-making authority – when a decision is required, the team can still adopt the decision-making process the leader has established. Nor does it mean that the group team leader loses control of the agenda because they must approve it.

When the leader decides to turn meeting chairpersonship to others, provide best practices training to the full team. Over the course of a number of meetings, rotate responsibility for chairing the meetings to different individuals. After everyone's had a turn, select one (or perhaps alternate two people) to chair meetings moving forward – the best choice is usually obvious. Another option is to have the full team assess performance and choose the chair through consensus. An added bonus - turning the chairpersonship over to subordinates is great for evaluating potential successors. They learn the ropes under your supervision and start establishing their presence as a meeting leader with the rest of the team.

An effective chair is a leader, facilitator, provocateur, and stabilizer, who can balance their own input with the need to encourage input from others while managing processes, logistics, etc. It's a key role that significantly affects the creation and productive use of strategic time.

Get a handle on email, text, phone, and other communications

Studies indicate executives receive well over 200 emails a day (almost half are irrelevant to them), and checking, reading, responding, and organizing them can eat up almost 15 hours per week. [6] Email is a powerful communication tool and taking better control of it offers potential opportunities for creating strategic time.

The first question to consider is, 'How important is email to me?' According to studies, people check 70% of emails within six seconds of receipt, and 85% check within two minutes.[6] Although it sounds like a priority for most people, half of those surveyed said that email is a major block to their productivity and checking it is primarily an addictive reaction.

For most people, email content usually isn't very important most of the time. Yet, I often see executives in senior team meetings pay more attention to email communication with people outside the room than face-to-face communication with those inside it. Most admit it's an example of misplaced priorities – a classic triumph of urgent/not important over important/not urgent.

The best way to avoid checking email is to turn off notifications when you're thinking strategically, attending meetings, etc. If you do need to be concerned about important/urgent issues, provide those involved with other ways of contacting you, such as text, or through an assistant who will track you down.

Another simple technique is to block parts of your day for email and avoid it all other times (unless it's truly urgent). Tell those you work with regularly that unless the subject line contains the word 'urgent', you won't be checking emails until a specified time. Most clients and other stakeholders are fine with this, provided you discuss it with them beforehand.

Some executives have an elaborate filing system for emails. I recommend simplicity – respond to urgent messages immediately, move non-urgent but important messages requiring a response or filing to a folder for review at a specified time, and abandon everything else. At the specified time, deal with them as needed.

If you like a clean inbox, go back and delete everything still there without opening. However, some like to hold on to old emails in case there's something they might need later, so they let them sit and periodically delete everything in their inbox older than three months. I use this technique and there's something liberating and pleasurable about deleting 2000 or so emails at once.

Previously I recommended avoiding email and voicemail until you've put in your strategic thinking time. However, as soon as it's complete, spend 15–30 minutes checking and sorting email in a block of time (at the end of morning and/or mid-afternoon). Resist being seduced into spending more time than you've allotted.

For those you communicate with regularly, text messaging is faster than email and much faster than phone. Reduce your intake of email messages by using filters that automatically categorize and bundle much of your email traffic, and look into collaborative/productivity enhancement tools like Slack, ActiveCollab, Microsoft Teams, Superhuman or Streak that greatly speed up and simplify communication within teams and beyond. For instance, to save time, many executives use collaborative tools to replace the bulk of their internal online communication, reserving email for external communication only.

One of the most frustrating (and time-consuming) activities associated with electronic organizers is scheduling meetings with others, especially if they're outside your organization and you can't access their Outlook calendar. An executive assistant greatly facilitates this task, however, if you don't have one try some of the emerging new smart calendar apps that enable you to coordinate all aspects of scheduling with participants internal or external to your organization.

As much as possible, when composing emails, limit content to fit in the subject line so messages don't have to be opened. Don't copy anyone who doesn't 'need to know'. Reply-all should only be used when absolutely necessary, because it's a distraction to those who don't need to see it and the less email you send the less you receive. Use dictation to speed up the production of long emails. Maintain a detailed signature line with current contact information so that others have alternate ways to respond without writing you for the information. Keep every email as short as possible – it encourages others to do the same.

Finally, have a conversation with those you communicate with regularly – your primary teams, direct reports, etc. – to establish 'rules of the road' with regard to email. For example, clarify things like when to copy and/or copy all, when extreme brevity is desired, and when delays to an email response are not personal, just an effort to manage email time, etc.

A final form of communication you'd be wise to manage as well as possible is status reports, especially regular, standardized ones. Many executives tell me they arrive at work on Monday morning facing four to eight reports from various departments, many of which they don't open because the information they contain is largely irrelevant and/or presented in a way that renders the report virtually unintelligible. How much time would you save if you eliminated those reports you don't read and had the others immediately redesigned or condensed? An added bonus – those who prepare the reports you eliminate can put their time and attention to more value-adding work.

Put all of these tactics to use, and don't be surprised if you turn a third of your email time into productive strategic time.

Reduce the time you commit to meetings

For a number of reasons – increases in the perceived benefit of collaborative dialogue, a desire for greater inclusion, proliferation in the access of easy-to-use scheduling software, etc. – the amount of time executives spend in meetings of three or more coworkers has been growing steadily since 2008.[(7)]

In addition, many executives feel compelled to attend meetings when asked because they want to be supportive, even when they know there's much more important things to be working on.

Because meetings represent such a significant part of an executive's schedule – many spend 50–60% of their time in meetings – liberally applying time-saving tools and techniques should easily free up three to four hours per week for more strategic endeavors.

A first tactic for reducing meeting time is to periodically review your calendar and stop attending those meetings – especially recurring ones – that no longer fit with your priorities and time allocations. Be rigorous – your attendance may add value, but can your time be better spent on higher-level initiatives? In fact, there may be other attendees who feel a particular meeting's run its course, and cancelling it outright might serve everyone.

Of course, a corollary to this is don't schedule meetings unless there's no reasonable alternative. Before booking, consider whether an email, call, or quick huddle in the hallway would get the same result in less time.

If there are some meetings you can't stop attending altogether, can you send someone in your place (another great developmental opportunity for someone more junior)? Alternatively, can you attend every second or third meeting or can you attend a part of the meeting, either the first half or last? Will a quick update email or a copy of the minutes allow you to stay in touch and react without committing the time needed to attend?

Most meetings are longer than they need to be. Try to shorten every meeting you schedule or attend. Scheduling programs automatically default to 30 or 60-minute blocks of time – perhaps one reason that about 60% of executive meetings are at least one hour long.

Strive to cut meeting time in half as much as possible, and make 15-minute meetings your default unless you really need more.

Resist the time others request for meetings; when asked for 30 minutes of your time, suggest you don't have it (even when you do), but can make 15 minutes available. Clearly, meetings involving strategic thinking or tackling a series of very difficult problems may need two to three hours (or longer) – don't render meetings ineffective in your quest for time. However, adopt the mindset that time is a critical resource (because it is), and always be on the lookout for opportunities to create it through shorter meetings.

Almost half of executive 'meetings' are two people communicating through email or phone. However, add a person and we're inclined to meet face-to-face even though technology easily accommodates meetings of any size. Face-to-face meetings have many advantages, but unfortunately they're the least efficient way to meet, waste time in booking, travelling to and from the meeting room (only to find the previous meeting's running late and everyone waits for the room to clear), and are most likely to start late.

Once everyone's arrived, more time is wasted socializing. Face-to-face meetings also promote common barriers to effective decision-making, such as groupthink, power imbalances shaping dialogue inappropriately, and unhelpful arguments and conflict (which are more common when meeting face-to-face and largely overcome with the use of technology). As a result, hold most meetings by phone or team applications like Zoom or Slack, etc. as much as possible unless face-to-face is truly necessary.

About half of all meetings start late. Bain estimates that a five-minute delay reduces the value of a meeting by 8% – waste most executives wouldn't routinely accept with any other organizational resource. [(7)] If you've cut meeting time in half, a five-minute delay is critical. If half of your meetings start five minutes late, that's about 75 minutes of strategic thinking time (or five 15-minute meetings) simply frittered away each week.

To combat late meetings, take a couple of minutes at your next meeting and have the chairperson state (restate) their expectations related to attendance, and have the group clarify the expectations they have for themselves – everyone wants meetings to start on time and it's easier to hold people accountable once expectations are stated and shared. This discussion often reveals the presence of scheduling or other issues that are contributing to tardiness – identify and remove them.

Once a few meetings start late, people assume it's standard practice (they've got a five to six-minute buffer) so best practice is to always start on time. If a meeting simply can't start because key people are missing, at the 'official' start time ask others if they'd like to start, or wait two minutes for others to arrive. If the answer is to wait, start the meeting exactly two minutes later – this procedure reinforces your commitment to timeliness and puts everyone on notice that the buffer is only two minutes.

At a meeting's conclusion, reinforce expectations for attendance and ask whether adjustments will ensure the next meeting starts on time. Add a note to meeting invitations stressing the importance of prompt arrival. Follow up with chronic late arrivers, restate expectations and the effect they're having on everyone else, and determine whether anything needs to change to help them meet expectations.

Put the agenda's most critical items at the start of the meeting and dive right into them so arriving a minute late means missing key information. A simple tool for getting everyone to the starting gate on time is tracking attendance or conducting a roll call. Quickly review agenda items and confirm the person responsible for each is prepared to address the issue. If a participant misses roll call, remove their item from the agenda. Give key participants an important speaking role at the start of the meeting; a 'safety moment' or 'innovation moment' or other topic important to the group. Finally, if lateness persists, as a last resort lock the meeting room door or close access to a teleconference call one minute after the meeting start time.

Insufficient meeting preparation forces many meetings to start late due to overbooked meeting rooms, inoperative teleconference dial-in numbers or passwords, issues with audio-visual setup, etc. Have an assistant or IT support team handle logistics, or assign responsibility to someone attending the meeting (perhaps on a rotational basis) or a junior member of your team.

Stop chairing meetings

The leader of the team usually assumes the role of meeting chairperson. When the job is done effectively it's time consuming, involving agenda development and other preparation, attendance at the meeting and post-meeting follow up, etc.

In the consulting business, we typically assume meeting preparation will take at least as long as the meeting itself, so a one-hour meeting takes one to two hours of preparation. As a result, giving the chair's role to others can reduce a leader's time commitment significantly.

In fact, it might mean they can skip some meetings or attend meetings partially, knowing things are in good hands. To facilitate this, remember that there are typically four roles in any decision: users provide input into decisions before they're made, evaluators provide advice/consultation to help decide between different options, decision-makers select options, and approvers sanction the decision after it's made. Strive to be an approver as much as possible.

The approver's role is advantageous because you don't have to research, consult with others or attend meetings, yet retain full control over the decision. This frees you to focus elsewhere and enables others to develop critical skills necessary in a decision-maker/approver relationship (similar to the governance relationship between the executive team and the board).

When you've been given responsibility for an initiative, resist the urge to join the group you'll form to take it on. Give decision-making authority to others, maintain oversight and approval, and use the time they set aside for meetings to think strategically about other, higher-level problems.

Start work earlier and start work thinking strategically

Recently, I joined an 8:00 a.m. meeting with a very effective executive who lives in a time zone four hours earlier than my own. At the end of the meeting I just had to ask if she was on the road (assuming she was in a time zone closer to my own). 'No,' was the reply, 'I start all my workdays at 4:00 a.m.'

When executives ask me how they can make more strategic time, my first question is, 'What time do you start work in the morning?' Answers vary, but when I hear 'between 8:00 or 9:00 a.m.,' my first response is 'go to work earlier in the morning.'

Waking up before 6:00 a.m. isn't natural for many people and unappealing when they're already working 60 to 65 hours a week (including weekends). Besides, there are impediments, for example, a one to two-hour morning commute might mean a 5:00 a.m. start just gets you to the office by 8:00 a.m., or you have pre-school responsibilities with young children.

These are legitimate concerns, however, starting work earlier offers significant rewards, especially when that time is focused on strategic thinking. For instance, it's the best opportunity to find a one to two-hour block of uninterrupted time. Early morning contemplation of big issues brings clarity, focus, and direction to the rest of your day.

In addition, strategic thinking is most effective before the hustle-bustle of our workdays start because it utilizes internal thought processes (referred to as 'top-down processing') that require attention controlled by the individual and primarily focused on memories and knowledge. In contrast, email, meetings, etc., utilize thought processes (referred to as 'bottom-up processes') where attention is under the control of external stimuli (we're directed by them whether we want to be or not). [8]

Bottom-up processing is detrimental to strategic thinking because once engaged, returning to top-down processing is difficult – our brains prefer bottom-up processing because it's easier to do. As a result, waking up earlier to engage in strategic thinking catches our mind when it's most open to top-down processing.

How do executives overcome barriers to starting work earlier? First, realize that waking up earlier is the best chance to find the blocks of uninterrupted time for top-down processing most conducive to strategic thought. Second, work very hard to maintain a regimen of early morning strategic time, a minimum of 10 hours per week (including weekends) dedicated to your most strategic initiatives (I wrote 80% of this book using this approach).

To strengthen your regimen, start working as soon as possible after waking up – grab a cup of coffee, hit the office (home or work) and start thinking strategically. It helps to lay your work out the night before and strongly resist the urge to check email, voicemail, sport scores or anything else that might engage bottom-up processing. In addition, disable distracting notifications on email, text, voicemail, and other notifications.

If you can't find one to two hours of relative solitude in your home office, instead of doing email, voicemail, etc. during your train or subway commute, think strategically. It's relatively easy to focus on top-down processing with light background noise (noise-cancelling headphones also help). Alternatively, use an earlier wake-up time to hit the gym and arrive at the office 30 to 60 minutes earlier for strategic thinking before the onslaught of meetings and distractions overtake you.

If you're simply an 'evening person' or can't possibly make an earlier start to your day, it's completely understandable, however, you'll have to find strategic time elsewhere in your schedule.

Maximize meeting time

In the good old days, most meeting distractions were initiated inside a meeting by participants who wouldn't stop talking or would take conversations off on wild tangents.

Those folks still exist and are now joined by distractions emanating from outside the meeting, such as computers, iPhones, iPads, and other devices connected to the internet. It's a significant source of distraction – about 25% of people compose and send three or more emails for every 30 minutes of meeting time. [7] When you consider that it takes the average person over a minute to fully reengage after an email distraction – research shows meeting distractions can have the same effect as a 10-point reduction in a person's IQ[9] – eliminating unnecessary distractions is an important time-saving tactic that also contributes to meeting effectiveness.

Distractions subvert the primary purpose of a meeting – to have people work together on a problem. If you can't limit distractions you might be better off having everyone go to their office and work on the problem alone.

Banning laptops and iPhones at meetings other than those necessary for presentations is tempting, however, it penalizes those who are using them for legitimate purposes like taking notes. Instead, discuss it with the full team and develop guidelines for managing the problem.

I've seen many groups readily agree that electronic equipment is permitted in meetings, however, ringtones, notifications, etc. must be turned to low or vibrate. If someone has to take a call or respond to an email, they'll notify the chairperson and leave the room, returning as quickly as possible, or if there's a pre-scheduled call or conversation planned during the meeting, they'll notify the chairperson beforehand so their absence can be accommodated with a change to the agenda.

No one likes distractions and their negative impact on meeting effectiveness and productivity, and most will willingly put up with restrictions on the use of technology as long as they apply to everyone and are flexible enough to account for extenuating circumstances when necessary.

Work with the best executive assistant (EA) you can

For years, I've had the distinct pleasure to be supported by a wonderful colleague (Shannon) who's managed me and my calendar (among other things). In the process, she's handled thousands of Tame problems I'd otherwise have had to address. I know executives who don't have a personal/executive assistant, and they're missing out on a truly essential time-creating resource.

Booking meetings and meeting rooms, making travel arrangements, editing and formatting documents, handling logistical details, managing email and calendars (including the defense of your strategic time allocations), and dozens of other time-creating activities are removed from your attention by an effective EA.

If you and/or your company can't afford a full-time EA, (and you need to seriously question whether this is the case, i.e. one might be made available on a part time basis) there are virtual assistants available online, such as Tasks EveryDay and NS Virtual Services that can help (to name just a couple, there are many others). Few of us can completely escape Tame problems in life, but every minute spent on them is a minute that might be productively and effectively utilized elsewhere.

Establish an efficient system for file and record management

With apologies to document management experts, for most of us filing is one of the least exciting topics in all management literature. Which might be why we spend so little time thinking carefully about how to optimize it.

That's a big problem because filing is essentially an extension of our brain – it's how we store all the information we can't or don't need to retain in our memory. As a result, accessing it as efficiently and effectively as possible is very important. Yet, how many times have you spent 10 or more minutes looking for an important file (hard or soft copy) without success? How many times have you worked on a document for hours only to realize the version you're using is outdated? How often have you saved a great idea from a workshop, conversation, website, Twitter, etc. to one of your many devices (phone, iPad, network drive, computer hard drive, portable USB and/or the cloud to name a few) to subsequently never find it again.

One study (validated by others) shows the average office worker can spend up to two hours/day looking for information[10]. That's hard to believe, but even if it's half true, it's an outrageous waste of time and productivity – time you could spend on more strategic pursuits.

To prevent that sort of time loss happening to you, apply a simple, proven structure to your personal filing/document management, especially digital files. There are a number out there (they're sometimes referred to as Personal Knowledge Management Systems) and they can significantly improve the ease and efficiency of file retrieval. The one I use is developed by Tiago Forte and goes by the acronym PARA: Projects (a series of tasks linked to a goal, with a deadline), Areas (a sphere of activity with a standard to be maintained over time), Resources (a topic or theme of ongoing interest), and Archives (inactive items from the other three categories). Everything I retain (on all my devices) rolls up under these four headings.

Using PARA, I don't have to remember where I've filed anything because the structure quickly and intuitively leads me to whatever I'm trying to find. PARA was very easy to learn and the time and frustration associated with file and document retrieval has virtually dropped to zero. It's remarkable that such a simple fix can lead to such big gains.

Conclusion

Resist the urge to simply work longer and harder, particularly over the long term. The typical executive is already overwhelmed, working very long hours, and the best way to make strategic time is by creating it. Scour your calendar for opportunities to drop and stop activities, say no to lower-level problems (so you can focus on higher-level ones), negotiate more strategic time and redesign key executive activities – especially meetings – so you're more effectively focused and productive. Identify low-hanging fruit and start creating immediately – create just enough time to think strategically about how you can create more time – because the longer you wait, the more good intentions can fade, the more frustrated you become, and the longer it takes to build strategic thinking and other capabilities critical to your executive role.

Topics we covered in Chapter 8 – Create strategic time – pull weeds.

Topic	Page
• Introduction	115
• Create strategic time – guiding principles	117
• Use to-do lists	117
• Go digital as soon as possible	118
• Delegation	119
• Dictation	120
• Better reading habits	120
• The primary purpose of team meetings – enable better decisions	122
• Put a value on time	123
• Reduce the number of people in meetings	123
• Clarify and agree on the decision-making process	126
• Keep people focused on the 'task at hand'	128
• Always have a qualified meeting chairperson	129
• Get a handle on email, text, phone, and other communications	131
• Reduce the time you commit to meetings	133
• Stop chairing meetings	136
• Start work earlier and start work thinking strategically	137
• Maximize meeting time	138
• Work with the best executive assistant (EA) you can	139
• Establish an efficient system for file and record management	140
• Conclusion	141

9 MANAGE STRATEGIC TIME – PREVENT WEED GROWTH

'Time is the scarcest resource and unless it is managed, nothing else can be managed.' – Peter Drucker

Introduction

THERE'S A STORY about J. Edgar Hoover that demonstrates the power executives can unwittingly wield over those they lead.

Apparently, because he reviewed many of his agents' reports, he mandated that they should never be more than two and a half pages long, with wide margins all around the text so he could make notes. An agent submitted a report that ignored this rule about the margins, and an exasperated Hoover scrawled, 'Watch the borders!' When subordinates saw the note, they assumed he meant the national borders with Mexico and Canada and sent hundreds of agents there.

This story illustrates how those reporting to any executive are continuously aware of the authority vested in the position. As a result, executives need to monitor the number and nature of directives they assign to direct reports and the time it takes to complete them.

That's not all. Executives (especially senior ones) are role models for the entire organization.[1] Getting entangled in the weeds and/or treating time like an unlimited resource sends signals sure to be mirrored by many others – actions speak louder than words.

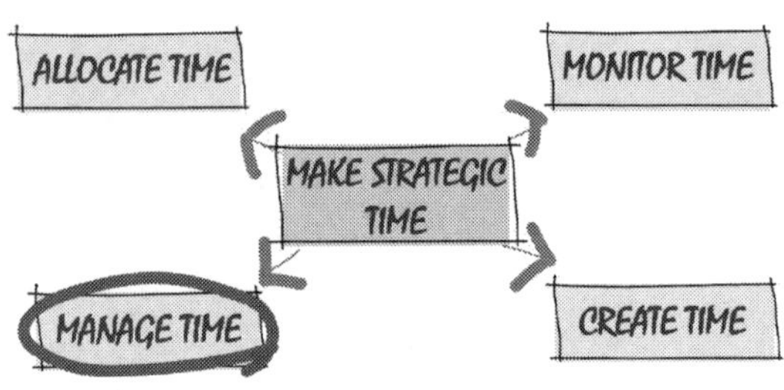

Managing strategic time is a recognition that time wasting is both a personal and organizational problem. Executives have a responsibility to ensure that their behaviors and decisions build a culture that honors the importance of time. Everyone's time is a critical organizational resource, and strategic time is a critical commodity for every executive.

Yet, there's evidence that time is not being managed well. For instance, the time it takes to hire new employees, a critical competitive function, has risen by almost 30% in just five years.[2] A 2011 Boston Consulting Group study found that over a 15-year period, the number of organizational functions increased between 50–350% (depending on organization or function).[3]

Clearly, most executives can do a better job of managing time. When they dedicate their own time to the wrong things, have little appreciation for how time is managed in their department or function, ignore time-wasting practices, unnecessarily delay decisions, or fail to consider the increased time most change forces on those they lead, they're mismanaging time and inadvertently making it impossible to create strategic time for themselves (and everyone else).

Manage strategic time – guiding principles

Before looking at strategies and tactics for managing time effectively, let's outline a few guiding principles:

- Time is a critical (finite) organizational resource – wasted time can erode shareholder value. As much as possible, decisions should ensure that time is always effectively utilized;
- The ineffective use of time can be reversed through better self and organizational management; and
- Executives are responsible for how well or poorly time is managed and utilized in an organization.

Develop well-functioning processes for strategy development and execution

Strategy development and execution is an executive's primary role, and their effectiveness is dependent on the quality and integrity of the processes that produce and operationalize good strategy.

Anyone who is stuck in a bad strategic process or wasting months on an ill-fated strategic initiative knows firsthand the hundreds (if not thousands) of employee hours wasted when bad strategic decisions combine with badly managed implementation. It's a recipe for organizational failure.

Strategy can break down in dozens of places – insufficient strategic thinking time, bad strategic thinking, misalignment between executives, lack of trust between executives and their direct reports, and implementation that fails to deliver on strategic intent (to name a few).

Bad strategic processes are a big reason why so few executives make strategic time. After all, a single executive can't affect organizational strategy on their own, so without a workable structure of processes and mechanisms to translate individual strategic thinking into collective dialogue, intention, and action, executives won't see the benefit of working on highest-level problems. Many think, 'Why bother?'

I believe one of the first steps to better strategy is establishing a regular pattern of meetings or dialogue that link strategic thinking to operational action. First, establish separate meetings for strategy development and operational execution. Ideally, operational meetings should be once a week and strategy meetings quarterly (at a minimum). The intent of operational meetings (usually 60–90 minutes long) is to ensure alignment between the strategic plan and strategic implementation; reviewing progress towards objectives and the timely resolution of significant issues.

Ideally, quarterly 'strategic dialogue' meetings (usually four to eight hours long) are used to revisit the key, high-level organizational elements, i.e. direction, strategy, operating model, etc. presented in Chapter 2. They can also be used to review progress on the strategic plan, make adjustments to current strategy in response to new operational or environmental developments, and initiate discussion on highest-level problems that have emerged subsequent to the strategic plan's development, etc.

In many organizations, this meeting is supplemented with a strategic dialogue on an 'as-needed' basis in the event an issue arises that can't wait for the quarterly meeting. It's a good idea to schedule a one or two-hour meeting between each quarterly meeting for this purpose, and cancel it when it's not needed. Another option is to schedule a 15-minute 'huddle' for a quick check-in to determine whether a longer meeting is needed.

Of course, none of this guarantees strategic thinking or ensures that dialogue will be effective, however, it provides a structure that stimulates a need for both and the time required to do it well.

Group/team behavioral agreements

Almost every executive is responsible for the effective management of one or more groups/teams and knows how badly dysfunctional teams drain productivity and time. A simple technique for helping address this problem is team agreements.

A team agreement is simply a code of conduct or list of behavioral norms meant to guide behavior. Because the group develops them together and agrees on their importance to group effectiveness, they make it easier for leaders (and others) to hold group members accountable for dysfunctional or unproductive behavior, especially when those behaviors are hard to confront under normal circumstances. Essentially, agreements are preventive maintenance against the corrosion that can result from group and interpersonal interaction over time, especially when people are under pressure.

Check online for processes you can use to build agreements (simplicity is key - any process that takes more than 15 minutes to conduct is unnecessarily complex). Once developed, I encourage groups to keep them handy (some include them with minutes or keep them posted in their meeting room) and revisit them periodically.

For instance, at the start of a meeting a leader might ask participants to quickly review the agreements they've created and identify one (or two) they feel are not currently being fully honored by the team. When there's consensus that one is deficient (the example on the right indicates four people feel there's a lack of candor), the leader asks for ideas that will get the level of candor back to desired levels.

The level of candor (honesty) has serious implications for team productivity. When it's high, people are more likely to 'take things on faith' and consent is relatively quick because issues and concerns are 'out in the open'. When it's low, this doesn't happen. Low candor often persists because people can't even be honest enough with one another to confront the problem – it's a reason almost 55% of executives feel their organization is less honest/candid as it should be[4] and some teams slog through years of low candor. Anyone who's worked in an environment like that knows how draining and time-wasting it is. Instead of letting this situation fester, agreements make it easier to get the subject on the table and resolve it before too much time, energy, and productivity is wasted.

Reduce VUCA wherever possible

We've already discussed how rising VUCA is contributing to organizational disruption. I increasingly see organizations, particularly ones that waited too long to react to highest-level problems, attempt to make up for lost time by adopting a 'hurry up and do something' energy that encourages a lot of wasted time and effort.

Every time an executive makes a change to anything, they eat up organizational time. Even good decisions require time-consuming effort for everyone affected. For instance, the executive must personally increase oversight, those reporting to them increase management of those they lead, their people spend time planning and implementing the change, other departments and/or functions in the organization spend time accommodating the change in their process and systems, and the change may further extend beyond the organization to touch customers, regulators, stakeholders, etc. Time is also spent mothballing old ways of working, learning new ways of working, correcting mistakes along the way, etc. In effect, the response to external disruption inevitably creates internal disruption that can distract hundreds (if not thousands) of employees from value-creating work with clients.

To reduce that internal disruption, work to ensure decisions create as little volatility as possible; evaluate how to achieve desired results without any change or by keeping the number of changes and scope of change as low as possible. Minimize unfamiliarity by limiting the introduction of radically different processes or new working and reporting relationships. Streamline reporting lines and authority to reduce complexity and make expectations, roles, etc. as clear as possible to manage ambiguity.

Most executives have a strong personality preference for change and see opportunities for improvement everywhere. If that sounds like you, remember that most organizational innovation is incremental, taking place over the normal course of doing business.

Big changes carry bigger risk of failure (most transformational change fails to deliver on expectations) [(5)] and reducing time wasted on unproductive change is often a case of increased impulse control, i.e. resisting your impulses unless the benefits minus change costs are greater than the status quo. Ask yourself, will this new work deliver more value than current work? How much time will it take to plan and implement this effectively? Is there another alternative that delivers acceptable results and uses much less time? Is the downside of doing nothing acceptable? If it is, consider doing that instead.

Stop distracting others

Before I started this book, I completed a strategic time survey by asking some CEOs if they'd have their teams invest three minutes to access it online. Many agreed and I'm very grateful.

One wrote back saying he would complete it himself but wouldn't forward it to the others because 'they're very busy right now and I don't want to distract them.' I like to think that every CEO made the same calculation, because my request was a classic high urgency/low importance distraction.

Asking a CEO for three minutes of his/her team's time seems innocuous, but consider that executives get dozens of similar requests a day, and that wasted time and energy adds up fast. Furthermore, these types of distractions disrupt priorities that are more important, and by creating them you're modeling behavior others are sure to emulate.

The tendency for easy distraction is personality related – I've had some executives refer to themselves as 'crows' because they're so easily attracted to 'every shiny object', and there's no question that a preference for experimentation, challenging the status quo, and risk-taking are (at the same time) valuable attributes and a recipe for being pulled in many directions at once.

However, executives must temper their urge for distraction, because direct reports are keenly responsive to their requests, even when they're whims – they'll often support you even when doing so isn't good for anyone. Be very careful what you ask for; too many distractions mean less time for value-adding priorities and strategic thinking.

Build your leadership capabilities

There's a direct relationship between time and leadership capability. The greater your capability, the less time it typically takes to accomplish things – experts are faster and more effective than novices in their area(s) of expertise.

In every organization, four levels of leadership capability correspond to the four levels of problem difficulty. At the lowest level (Team level), leaders focus primarily on leading team members from their own department or function. At the next level (Multi-Discipline level), they focus on leading cross-functional (multi-discipline) and/or departmental teams. At the third level (Enterprise level), they lead across the whole business, and at the fourth (Industry level), they extend their leadership out into their industry or beyond.

At the Team level, leaders primarily gain followership through their strong technical or functional expertise. However, at the Multi-Discipline level, especially when leading cross-functional efforts with others of equal or greater authority, leadership capability becomes as important as technical expertise. At higher levels, it's even more important.

As executives advance from one level to another the nature of behaviors necessary for effectiveness change dramatically – 'what got you here won't get you there' is an accurate axiom. Yet many executives don't make sufficient time needed for the development of new leadership capabilities as they advance in seniority.

For example, consider the leader capability of 'influence'. Influence is the ability to 'get others onside' with your ideas when you don't have authority over them. At the Team level, leaders presenting the most logical arguments or business cases tend to prevail. They're then promoted to a Multi-Discipline level with others who share this capability – at this level, those who can differentiate their logical arguments with the use of persuasion tend to prevail.

At the Business and Enterprise levels, most people are able to make logical, persuasive arguments, and it's those who have developed the ability to build relationships and use political acumen that tend to prevail.

At the most senior organizational levels, leaders who regularly combine logic, persuasion, relationship development, and political acumen are the most capable influencers.

This same progression in skills applies to every leadership capability. Unfortunately, most executives don't discover they're deficient (unconsciously incompetent) in key areas of capability until after they've been promoted, creating management deficiencies that sap everyone's time. For instance, lack of capability reduces the confidence others have in your decision-making and breeds mistrust – factors that reduce productivity.

Leadership capability is at the core of an executive's effectiveness, particularly when they begin leading in multi-disciplinary environments. Making the time for continuous development is an ongoing, life-long necessity for every executive, especially when the environment is disruptive.

Just do it – start a strategic dialogue

Of course, a powerful way to make strategic time is to book a meeting with your full senior team and have a strategic dialogue (or maybe you start with a sub-set of the team and enroll the full team ASAP). I've found that once engaged, executives find strategic dialogue to be uplifting, challenging and fulfilling. After all, for many, it's why they relished becoming executives in the first place – they desperately want the opportunity to step back, see the full picture and begin exploring the biggest problems and opportunities. They want to test and push themselves and make a tangible, positive difference.

As a result, when I work with executive teams, an early step in my 'process' is to ask some big questions that stimulate exploration and problem-solving. Unsurprisingly, the first ones mirror the high-level organizational elements I introduced in Chapter 2.

- What is this organization's purpose? What impact (if any) does the disruption we'll face have on our purpose?

- What is this organization's direction? What is the 'picture' of the organization we want/must attain in three to five years (or longer) to successfully advance our purpose?

- What are the key strategies that will best realize the direction we seek? What must we change about our current strategy to successfully navigate the disruption we face now or will face in the future?

- Given our strategies, what is the operating model that will best carry us forward? What must we change about our current operating model to successfully navigate the disruption we'll face in pursuit of our direction?

- Given our operating model, what are the skills and capabilities we need in key leadership positions? What leadership skills and capabilities must we add (must I add in my department) to navigate the disruption we'll face in pursuit of our direction?

- What are the key cultural attributes we must consistently exhibit to execute our strategies and realize our direction? What must be done to resolve (as effectively as possible) current or anticipated misalignments between the culture we want and the one we have?

- What impact do changes to any/all of the high-level organizational elements above have on our current operational plans?

- What are the three biggest problems/risks we face right now that must be resolved in order for us to move forward as effectively as possible?

- What's the first step and key subsequent steps we must take to build and fully align around solutions to these questions?

I typically start with the question on purpose and proceed sequentially through each. The length of time needed for dialogue depends on a number of factors, for instance, little is needed if the team has recently explored some/all of the questions and considerable dialogue may be needed if they haven't.

This dialogue is not intended to develop complete and final answers. It's primarily intended to: a) get executives talking together about these big questions - stimulate strategic thinking; b) identify early thinking and areas where additional information and dialogue is required (prompting a thorough scan of the external/internal environment); and c) stimulate an intention for regular dialogue.

Build your political acumen

If you've ever had your department or function dedicate significant time to a key strategic initiative only to find you're unable to get support for it at the executive table, you've experienced firsthand the negative impact low influencing capability can have on your time and effectiveness.

I've previously mentioned the need for executives to continually develop capabilities as they elevate in the organization. Although all leader capabilities are important, Deloitte research [(6)] reveals influencing and political skills are the least developed 'mental model', representing a key source of ineffectiveness, particularly among senior executives.

Politics is ultimately a fight for the allocation of resources – capital, authority, and people among others – and plays an essential role in executive effectiveness. Without influencing/political capability, executives struggle to get stakeholders and colleagues onside with their ideas or advocate effectively for their department, even when their ideas make sense.

Influence is key to political acumen, and unlike the exercise of authority, it takes significant skill and time to conduct effectively. Compare the difference in effort between 'telling' someone to do something and: identifying the internal and external people you need to get onside; building and managing new relationships; establishing coalitions, conducting trade-offs; and persuading, positioning, pressuring, cajoling and tracking relationships in networks as they shift over time. Not to mention the time needed to build leverage through a combination of networking, information gathering, information provision, doing favors, showing interest, etc.

It's exhausting to read, let alone carry out consistently. You simply can't do it well if you can't stay out of the weeds and allocate the significant strategic time needed to do it right.

Ensure your key people always have one strategic initiative

In Chapter 6, I wrote about how important it is for you to have at least one significant strategic initiative on your plate at all times. The same applies to those reporting to you. If your top people aren't approaching you with strategic ideas, go to them and assign at least one initiative that pulls them out of the weeds.

We've seen before that a great deal of an employee's effort is discretionary, and there are few more inspiring ways to tap into that effort than providing opportunities to elevate the capability to solve higher-level problems and advance. This simple exercise advances your agenda and organizational value and creates development opportunities. Done well, it motivates your direct reports to improve their delegation capability and work to raise the performance of those reporting to them – a win-win proposition that elevates your whole department.

Pulling those you lead into more strategic endeavors is also an opportunity to coach or mentor others in the capabilities needed to think strategically. In Chapter 5, I talked about the ability of mental models or schemas to accelerate learning. Introduce your team to the mental models associated with strategic thinking, and use them to guide their learning and efforts. In addition, use these projects as an opportunity to clarify expectations with your key people, and model how you intend to hold them accountable for meeting those expectations.

Remember, strategic thinking is a learned capability that relies on the experience gained through on-the-job application and practice. Start preparing your key direct reports for a future of strategic thinking ASAP.

Executive transition labs

A big reason many executives hit the road on a new job and immediately head towards a ditch is the unfortunate state of most executive onboarding programs. Studies have shown that executive onboarding and transition efforts have failure rates of 25–40%.[7] Of course, while the executive is struggling, their department is also spinning their tires.

The principal reasons for failure are related to ineffective focus; new executives fail to address highest-level problems, particularly the cultural and political environment,[7] because they're so often pushed into the weeds.

Transition labs are a relatively new mechanism for helping executives transition to new roles and get on track fast. For instance, Deloitte (among other companies) offers transition labs to new senior executives that get the executive focused on highest-level problems right out of the gate, developing specific plans for cultural and political integration and helping to initiate a 100-day plan that accelerates learning and impact.

Simplify organizational structure

Organizational structure is a key component of the organization's operating model and establishes how activities are directed in order to achieve the goals of the organization.

At the extremes, organizations are either decentralized or centralized, however, most organizations are hybrid models that attempt to balance the advantages and disadvantages of each. For instance, as you increase decentralization, the speed and flexibility of decision-making tends to increase, but economies of scale and product or service continuity decrease. As you increase centralization, you address these disadvantages, but decision-making becomes slower and more rigid (more bureaucratic).

Executives are responsible for approving the organizational structure, and they're often shifting it to get a design that best supports the pursuit of goals and strategies. Due to rising VUCA, organizational redesigns are happening a lot more often – a 2012 recent survey revealed that 90% of companies with more than 1000 employees had restructured.[8]

However, because organizational structure also delineates reporting lines, span of control, roles and responsibilities, working relationships, processes, etc., even small shifts can demand significant time and effort to implement. Unless the redesign is truly necessary and successfully delivers on desired outcomes (50–75% fail to deliver desired outcomes), [9] this is wasted time.

Even when successfully implemented, designs can significantly increase time wastage by increasing the number of reporting relationships, approvals, and interactions between individuals. As organizations decentralize, many employees find themselves in 'matrix' relationships, reporting to two people (at a minimum) and responsible for keeping three to six others regularly informed. It's little wonder that about 60% of employees now interact with 10–20 or more people daily in the normal course of their work and 30% must interact with 20 or more[(10)] – much of it low-value work.

The purpose of this section isn't to dive too deeply into the subject of organizational design – there are excellent consultants and books that do just that. My intention is to shine a light on how significantly organizational design affects the use of time.

Bad design institutionalizes time-wasting practices. Good design starts with alignment on organizational purpose, direction, a clear organizational strategy, and constant attention to the principle that limiting interactions between people increases productivity and the effective use of time.

Effectively manage the strategic development time you do have

Is there anything more frustrating than successfully solving the wrong problem? Your executive team has invested significant time and effort diagnosing, analyzing, deciding on and implementing a solution – at great cost and effort – only to find the situation persists because you misdiagnosed the problem.

The potential for misdiagnosis increases significantly as VUCA rises. As a result, when it comes to Wicked and Extra-Wicked problems, it's not unusual to spend more time in problem-definition than problem-solving.

This is especially true for teams. Because highest-level problems are usually too difficult for individuals to solve alone, they're tackled collectively. However, a group of people can't solve a problem collectively unless everyone's aligned on the problem – until that happens, everyone's thinking strategically about a different problem.

This sounds obvious, but my research on strategic time reveals that only half of executives say their senior team is aligned on the organization's top three highest-level problems. Personally, my experience tells me most only think they're aligned. I've asked many senior teams to identify the highest-level problems faced by the organization, and it's clear with most of them it's not something they've recently discussed.

Worse, when individual team members name their highest-level problem, they usually identify symptoms – solving symptoms doesn't help when more fundamental or underlying problems are causing them.

Because highest-level problems are tough, we encourage senior teams to regularly align on the organization's three biggest problems, commit the strategic time required to effectively tackle them, and utilize processes that maximize collective problem-solving capability.

To tackle highest-level problems, I recommend a process similar to the one I use with executive teams. It's adapted from a process developed by The Collaborative Operating System. [11] It starts with a review of the symptoms (those things that tell us there's a problem) and an exhaustive dialogue that results in a clear problem statement. Only then does the group move to solutions that delineate desired outcomes and a plan for achieving each of them.

Highest-level problem-solving is enhanced when executive teams consistently exhibit four attributes. First, patience. Most executives like to move to solution as quickly as possible, however, they must resist the urge to jump to conclusions before they've accurately defined and aligned on the problem.

Second, breadth. Research shows when given a list of potential solutions, people do a relatively good job making the best choice. However, they often fail to give themselves enough alternatives. To counter this, if you generate five potential solutions, challenge yourself to develop five more. This stimulates abstract thinking, creativity, broader exploration, and more options.

Third, diversity of thought. Our personality and experience affect the way we approach problems. However, because people with similar personality preferences self-select to similar careers and industries, members sharing common personality traits and backgrounds often dominate executive teams. Deploy techniques that increase diversity of thought, i.e. gather input outside the team, especially with those who strongly oppose the team's position.

Finally, ensure that there is a working system of meetings or interactions that help translate strategic thinking into sound strategic decisions.

Manage the use of collaboration and collaborative efforts

It seems everywhere you turn someone is extolling the virtues of collaboration and collaborative decision-making as it's commonly credited with increasing innovation, speed to market, improved stakeholder alignment, etc.

It's true that collaboration has the potential to support highest-level problem solving because it helps introduce diverse thinking into a discussion and can help facilitate innovation by breaking down departmental or functional silos.

However, it's also true that the time managers contribute to collaborative events has risen 50% in the past 20 years [(12)] even though the costs of collaboration have begun to exceed the benefits. [(13)] In fact, collaboration appears to significantly increase the time strain on the organization's best people (with most 'collaboration' happening between two people within a department, not across departments).[(14)]

The first step in managing collaboration effectively is getting clear about its three different meanings. Collaborative effort is working cooperatively with colleagues (someone else in their own department, function, office, etc.) or other department(s). The focus here is on increasing the quality of the interaction without increasing the time commitment. Unfortunately, there's often a big increase in interactions without a corresponding increase in tangible business results.

Collaborative decisions (we covered different methods for decision-making in Chapter 8) are those made collectively by a full group or team. The focus here is on a method for decision-making, and while the process does entail additional time commitment, it's minimal when managed properly.

Collaboration is working with one or more other people in another part of the business (department, function, office, etc.) to produce a business result you cannot produce on your own. Here, the purpose of collaboration is the production of a unique, tangible business outcome. The pursuit of financial returns is important because we're more likely to maintain effective collaboration when there's a tangible financial payoff.[15] Without producing tangible results, collaboration wanes and organizations can throw thousands of hours at bringing groups from different departments together to little or no avail.

In my view, when an executive has a sound working knowledge of overseeing collaboration between different parts of the business and has effectively trained direct reports to successfully identify collaborative opportunities and manage their implementation, they're a good idea. Otherwise, they can become a sinkhole where time and productivity are lost.

Manage the use of groups, committees, and teams

Technology has made it easy for anyone to organize a meeting whenever they like – there isn't another organizational resource that's treated as cavalierly as meeting time. For instance, do you know how many hours your people spent in meetings last month? Do you know whether those hours were well spent?

Meetings can run amok. For instance, the average mid-level manager has about 62 meetings a month (approximately 35% of their time – for many senior executives it's often higher) and it's estimated that almost 70% of that time adds little value to the organization. [16]

The biggest time wasters are formal groups or teams, especially the senior executive team. One study showed for every hour an executive spends in a senior team meeting, over 40 hours of time has been spent by subordinates in preparation. [17] It only makes sense to formalize a group when most of the problems its members face are too difficult to solve on their own because groups place a huge drag on productivity and time – as a general principle, the more formal the group, the more time is wasted.

Employees should require approval before forming groups,

committees, and teams, or conform to guidelines established beforehand. The overall principle – solve problems as quickly and informally as possible.

For instance, before a committee, group, or team is formed, the 'leader' should determine whether the group's primary purpose is sharing information, consultation, coordination, or decision-making, based on the specific objectives he/she is trying to achieve. The first three purposes can often be satisfied through the use of technology or coordinating and consulting with one another on an as-needed basis in small subgroups.

When a more formalized group is truly necessary, assess the difficulty and frequency of the problems they're likely to face before deciding on group formation. For high problem difficulty combined with moderate frequency, use ad hoc formal groups or standing workgroups. Conversely, when high problem difficulty combines with high frequency, consider the use of a standing team.

Except for standing teams, ensure that groups have an expiry date, otherwise they may keep meeting after initial objectives have been met because of habit or the establishment of new objectives that might not need the full group's involvement.

Keep groups/teams as small as possible (we talked about ideal team sizes in Chapter 8). This may mean establishing a small core group of members who attend every meeting with ad hoc members joining as needed.

The initial formation of a team is their least efficient and effective time (the famous forming and storming stages) because norm setting, relationship development, the establishment of processes and systems, etc. consume time without producing tangible results. To counter this, combine people who have worked together successfully in the past so they hit the ground running. As much as possible (I know this is a controversial topic worthy of a full book) consider and monitor the impact of 'rogue' team members very closely. It can be a very tough choice between the highly productive individual who can't get on with others, i.e. can't be trusted or can't align, and the productivity of the full team. I've personally seen many rogue team members eat up time and cripple productivity in situations that demanded high team effectiveness.

When was the last time you conducted an inventory of informal and formal groups operating in your part of the organization? Have someone assemble a list of all groups – ad hoc and standing – identifying the name of the chairperson, names of group members, and purpose of the group, including primary objectives and anticipated expiry date.

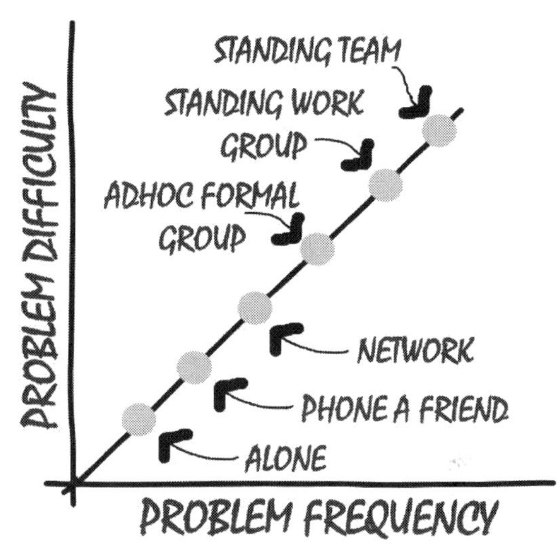

Finally, ask group/team leaders to suggest how the group could disband and still accomplish its objectives or (if it must meet) how they could cut meeting time in half. This final question might feel controversial, however, there are many tangible and intangible benefits to forcing shorter meetings.

First, it gives attendees an opportunity to reallocate the time to higher value work. When a meeting of seven people runs 30 minutes shorter, it frees three and a half hours of organizational time – if the meeting occurs once per week, that's 14 hours (two seven-hour days) of time available for higher-value work each month.

Second, it focuses attention on activities like decision-making that benefit most from face-to-face interaction and forces participants to conduct information sharing, consultation, and coordination in smaller groups as pre or post-meeting work.

Third, it helps leaders identify those direct reports able to make short, succinct, and persuasive arguments in less time – a key skill as you elevate in an organization – and those needing further development (as well as those unlikely to develop that skillset).

Fourth, it's another step towards building a culture that values strategic time.

You might get initial pushback as you reduce meeting time. If you do, remind people that almost 50% of employees consider meetings to be a significant waste of time and that there's good evidence to show they'd probably be more productive if they completely banned meetings for one day a week.[18]

Improve performance and talent management

Most time-management experts will advise a key tactic for freeing up your own time is to delegate more. However, when executives are asked why they're not making strategic time, their most popular reason is the inability to confidently delegate to direct reports. This inability suggests two issues: the current level of talent isn't up to the task, usually the result of ineffective talent management in the past, and/or executives aren't trained well enough in performance management to delegate effectively.

Talent management is a set of integrated processes designed to ensure the organization has the talent it needs in the *future*. Performance management is ensuring *current* performance is consistently rising. If you can't delegate now, you'll have the same problem tomorrow and an even bigger one three years from now, unless you address both.

If you aren't prepared to dedicate time to performance and talent management, you must be prepared to spend time dealing with ineffective employees and the negative effect they have on others – it's a lot of time.

For instance, a 2018 survey revealed managers spend up to 10 hours per week dealing with ineffective employees. [19] Of course, the impact of ineffective employees goes well beyond the manager's time to address them. In the same survey, over 90% of managers thought that ineffective employees 'somewhat or greatly' affect the broader team's morale in a negative way. Furthermore, about half of employees say poor performers increase the work burden of top performers and contribute to a lack of initiative and motivation [19] – they clearly have a detrimental impact on current performance and results.

I am struck by the time and emotional energy many executives expend on low-performing direct reports – it's not unusual for that dissatisfaction (and agonizing over what to do) to last months, sometimes years. Yet, once they take action, 100% say 'I wish I hadn't waited so long.'

As a result, I always suggest that executives bring the matter of a consistently underperforming direct report to a head as soon as possible. This doesn't mean taking immediate action, instead reflect on the following three questions:

1. As you envision your team one to three years into the future, do you see this individual having a role?

2. When the answer is yes, ask: can you address their shortcomings through development and/or a change in your behavior? When the answer is yes, design and initiate a development plan ASAP.

3. When the answer is no, ask: what's the deadline for replacing this individual and the plan that gets you there? Do they move to another role inside the organization or leave altogether and someone else moves into their role?

As soon as the team leader starts making a plan, there's relief that comes from resolving a troubling situation and having a simple process for taking action. I suggest leaders apply these three questions to each of their direct reports on a quarterly or semi-annual basis to proactively manage performance or talent concerns that erode valuable time and energy for all concerned.

Of course, there are many additional things executives can do to improve performance and talent management effectiveness. My intention isn't to explore them all, it's to highlight the importance of these two functions in your efforts to make more strategic time for yourself and others in your organization.

To accelerate your ability to delegate, always be trying to 'replace yourself' so you've got people ready to take on responsibilities you want to leave behind as you elevate to higher-level problems. To facilitate this, focus attention and development on your one or two highest performing direct reports. In particular, identify a 'most likely' successor and test/train them by delegating stretch opportunities to them.

Finally, accelerate development – yours and theirs – as much as possible. You have to make the first move. You can't delegate responsibilities to others until you let them go. Before you're 100% ready, allocate time for higher-level priorities and offload some of your responsibilities to others before they're 100% ready. This enables you to elevate sooner and forces you both to apply learnings directly to your work – the best way to develop.

Always be building a culture that values time

I'm always surprised when executives say a value-adding idea or practice can't be implemented because 'it goes against our culture.' Culture exists to support behaviors that add value to the organization, and when it fails to do that, it's an executive's responsibility to shift the culture.

No one has more of an effect on organizational culture than executives, especially senior executives. After all, they control the primary high-level inputs, i.e. organizational direction, strategy, operating model, etc. They also oversee the development of policies, procedures, processes, and resources that support culture. Wherever they go in the organization, they're seen as 'leaders', and others take cues from them that inform their own behavior. As a result, when executives effectively make strategic time or implement time-making tactics, they're making time for themselves and building a culture that does the same for everyone else. When they're in a constant state of overwhelm, show up late (or not at all for meetings), and perpetually focus on the wrong problems, etc. they're still building culture, just not the one they want.

It's easy to forget that culture isn't an immovable force or a bland corporate aspiration, it's 'the way we really do things around here' – the sum total of behaviors an organization's people consciously and unconsciously exhibit daily. Reflect for a moment on your own department or function and ask, 'Do we have a culture that truly values time, or is there more we can do to nudge it in that direction?'

If more can be done, grab one or two ideas/practices from this book and start shifting culture by using them ASAP.

Manage your 'First and Second Team' as effectively as possible

Everyone knows how the mismanagement of a group or team can waste time and productivity – bad decisions, lack of alignment, and wasteful meeting practices are just a few common issues. It's one of the reason this book dedicates so much time to ideas and practices that improve team effectiveness, especially when participants meet together.

Most teams don't perform as well as they should. For instance, research by Deloitte shows that only 12% of teams rate themselves as high performing.[20] Another study reveals that almost half of all teams fail to exceed expectations the organization has for their performance.[21]

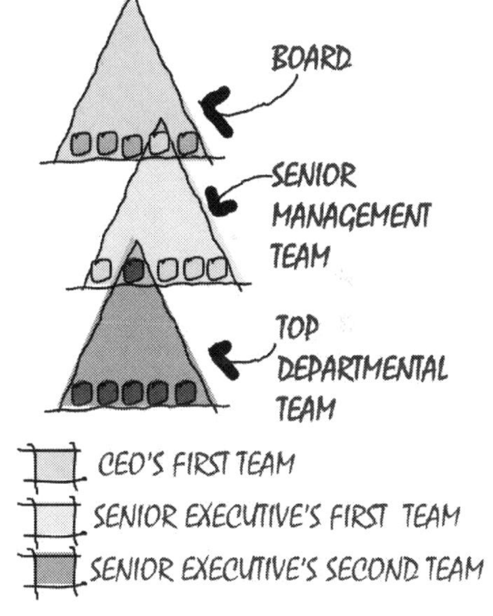

Over 90% of employees (even higher for executives) sit in two or more teams. [21] While an executive should do what they can to improve them all (it's part of building culture and overall productivity), time and energy are limited, so there are two teams that deserve the bulk of their attention: their First and Second Team.

Everyone in the organization has a First and Second Team. Their First Team[22] is the most senior team they're a member of in the organization. For example, the CEO's First Team is the board, and for senior executives, it's the organization's senior team. Your First Team gets your primary allegiance and focus and as much of your strategic time as possible because it's where the high-level organizational elements like direction, strategy, etc. that drive value are developed.

The Second Team is the most senior team an executive leads in the organization. For senior executives, it's usually the department/functional team they oversee because the strategies an executive's responsible for implementing are primarily delivered by this team (sometimes in concert with other departments). For executives or employees reporting directly to senior executives, this team is their First Team.

Why should these two teams get an executive's primary attention? Because executives get their direction from their First Team and implement it with their Second Team – bad direction from the First Team or misalignment between the teams makes good implementation by the Second Team very difficult. It also creates loads of time wasting and unproductive activity.

What can you do to improve effectiveness on these two critical teams? The first step is to ensure that the First Team is clear on its purpose. If not, it will continually corrupt the Second Team.

In addition, be sure you understand where your primary focus and allegiances lie – many executives see their Second Team as their primary team because it heads the department they lead. However, the needs and priorities of the First Team take precedence over their Second Team, and one of an executive's primary responsibilities is to make the knowledge and expertise resident in their Second Team readily available to First Team members.

Finally, focus your attention on getting these two teams to function as effectively as possible – when they don't, they corrupt all other teams that flow from them in the organization. Time wasting and unproductive practices or decisions in these two teams multiply exponentially.

Ask your people what's driving them into the weeds and what you can do to help

Even when an executive's intention is to manage in a way that honors the value of time, they sometimes unwittingly create the opposite effect. Here's a question any executive can ask their direct reports to help alleviate that concern – 'What's one thing I can do to help you make better use of time?'

The more senior an executive becomes in an organization, the less feedback they receive. A 2003 study showed that only 50% of employees are comfortable raising issues or concerns with their boss.[23] So it's no surprise that bosses are often in the dark about the time-killing impact they're having on their people.

Using the simple question above to ask for feedback helps overcome reluctance, and focusing on 'one thing' increases the odds you'll hear what each individual feels is the most important thing. After gathering as much feedback as you need, inform the group of the one or two initiatives you feel will have the greatest impact and the action you intend to take with a deadline for completion. Under promise and over deliver – the key is taking action.

Periodically check with the team to gauge progress and/or have them provide feedback at any time. Once the group feels you've successfully followed through, ask them again, 'What's the next thing I can do to help you make better use of time?'

Once you've demonstrated success with this approach, ask your direct reports to repeat this exercise with their direct reports. Typically, it isn't long before productivity and strategic time elevate.

According to a recent study,[24] when you ask your people for those things that most drive them into the weeds, in addition to unnecessary meetings, expect to hear about three areas employees find particularly time-wasting: needless administrative tasks, unproductive work conversations, and tasks associated with outdated or overly complex technology. It's the rare organization that's handling these areas as well as they should, so targeted interventions in one or more area will likely increase productivity and employment satisfaction.

Of course, there will be situations where direct reports are comfortable working in the weeds, and they may not be forthcoming with ideas aimed at increasing time or productivity. In this situation, some executives ask direct reports to prepare a 'downturn report' that identifies the decisions they'd make to change operations in the face of a real or hypothetical

15–20% downturn in business. These reports inevitably identify potential opportunities to streamline processes, eliminate bottlenecks and increase productivity.

Conclusion

As an executive, your organizational authority can waste an enormous amount of time – yours and others'. You're a role model and culture setter, and your attitude toward strategic time is one all those you lead will seek to emulate. In a world of rising VUCA and disruption, the impulse for change is overwhelming and even small ones lead to a litany of lower-level problems that can distract from more value-creating initiatives – you have to carefully balance the need for change with the need for stability. Time is a non-renewable resource and it's part of your executive role to ensure it's managed as closely and effectively as all other critical organizational resources.

Topics we covered in Chapter 9 – Manage strategic time – prevent weed growth.

Topic	Page
• Introduction	143
• Manage strategic time – guiding principles	144
• Develop well-functioning processes for strategy development and execution	145
• Group/team behavioral agreements	146
• Reduce VUCA wherever possible	147
• Stop distracting others	149
• Build your leadership capabilities	149
• Just do it – start a strategic dialogue	151
• Build your political acumen	153
• Ensure your key people always have one strategic initiative	154
• Executive transition labs	154
• Simplify organizational structure	155
• Effectively manage the strategic development time you do have	156
• Manage the use of collaboration and collaborative efforts	158
• Manage the use of groups, committees, and teams	159
• Improve performance and talent management	162
• Always be building a culture that values time	164
• Manage your 'First and Second Team' as effectively as possible	165
• Ask your people what's driving them into the weeds and what you can do to help	166
• Conclusion	168

10 STIMULATE SUCCESS AND DIAGNOSE FAILURE

Introduction

WHEN IT COMES to making strategic time, it's safe to assume there'll be barriers to success. Possibly lots of them. After all, if making strategic time was easy, over 90% of executives wouldn't be struggling to do it, and I wouldn't be writing this book.

Anticipating struggle and potential failure, this chapter is intended to help you: a) build habits that support your efforts to make strategic time and b) diagnose failures and get back on track ASAP. I included this chapter because I often work with executives and/or executive teams struggling to make strategic time, and these simple tips and processes help stimulate progress and overcome barriers.

If some of these ideas feel overly prescriptive and you've had lots of success shifting behavior in the past, you probably don't need them.

Getting started – make it habitual

A habit is a regular tendency or practice we consistently and (usually) unconsciously engage in over a long period of time. Of course, we all exhibit a few 'bad' habits. We may regularly show up a couple of minutes late for meetings or need to have the 'last word', etc. But we also have hosts of beneficial habits that enhance our life, such as rising early in the morning, following daily routines, smiling when someone does us a favor, etc.

The beauty of a 'good' habit is that, once established, we engage in the positive, helpful behavior it stimulates without sacrificing valuable cognitive space – it happens automatically. There are many great books on the establishment of habits. I've included a few ideas here to get you started.

Don't boil the ocean – seek small, steady improvement

I've previously mentioned the importance of taking one idea and implementing it as soon as possible – preferably right now or (at the latest) by end of day – for three reasons: a) it's easier to do one thing than two or more things; b) building competence doesn't start until you take action; and c) I want you to experience how liberating it feels to get at least one foot (even if it's just the small toe on your left foot) out of the weeds.

Another reason is that small, incremental improvements add up fast. As famed basketball coach John Wooden writes, 'When you improve a little each day, eventually big things occur. Seek the small improvement one day at a time. That's the only way it happens and when it happens it lasts.' Getting 1% better at something each day means you're 37 times better at it after one year.

Revolutionary personal manifestos or sweeping proclamations that radically shift behavior are great if you can pull them off. Most can't, but everyone can make and repeat one small change that over time creates a very big difference. For instance, it took two minutes for me to download a great to-do-list app with an immediate and discernable impact on productivity (and peace of mind). The next day, I cut a 1-hour weekly meeting in half, gaining two hours of strategic time per month.

Beware conscious incompetence

Remember the Conscious Competence Model from Chapter 3 and the conscious incompetence stage (upper left corner), where you know how to do something but can't do it well (yet)? This is the stage of change and self-improvement most people fail to survive because you know what you're trying to do but can't do it yet. If you've ever quit something in frustration, you likely called it quits at this stage of learning, before you had the chance to fully see the light at the end of the tunnel and reach unconscious competence – in the parlance of writer James Clear, you hadn't crossed the 'Plateau of Latent Potential.'[1]

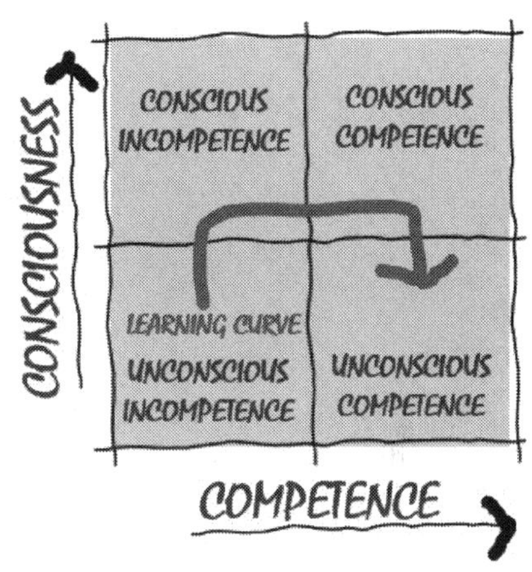

He writes, 'Complaining about not achieving success despite working hard is like complaining about an ice cube not melting when you heated it from 25 to 31 degrees. Your work was not wasted; it is just being stored. All the action happens at 32 degrees.' How long does it take for a habit to form? According to a 2009 study by Phillippa Lally, it depends on the person and their circumstances, but generally takes between 18 and 254 days – on average, habits form in 66 days.[2] This is much longer than the oft-heard 21 days and underlines the need to set your expectations for a (likely) two-month period of conscious and consistent practice before new routines are firmly established and strategic time allocations are fully realized.

Deploy a system that uses the whole strategic time model

Many people begin making strategic time by envisioning clear time allocations – goals they hope to achieve with time allocated to achieve them. Others start with monitoring their time more closely to gauge where it's currently going. Some don't start with either of those actions and start by creating more time

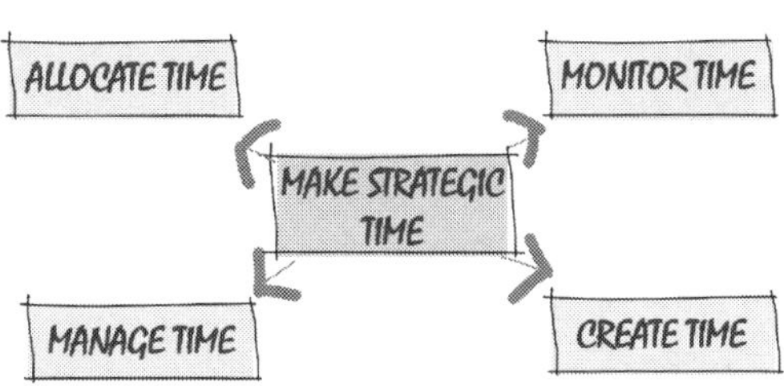

in their calendars or reducing management decisions that drive them and others into the weeds.

In isolation, none of these will consistently get the job done, so develop a simple system where each gets regular attention – ideally on the same date and same time of day. For instance, on one Saturday per quarter, check your allocations and make adjustments if necessary. Each Sunday evening, review your schedule for the week to get a sense whether it broadly aligns to your allocations and whether changes are needed, such as pushing something off to another week. To make sure you're tracking time through the week, use a calendar reminder to record your time at 12 p.m. and 5 p.m. each day. Alternatively, associate time entry with something else you have to do at those times, for example 'When I return from lunch I'll take two minutes to enter time' or 'When I pack my laptop to head home at the end of the day, I'll enter time and check my calendar for tomorrow.'

Schedule a five-minute calendar audit at the same date and time once per month or quarter to monitor progress against your allocations. Put a recurring reminder in your to-do list (easy to do with an app), to take a couple of minutes once a week to consider how you might introduce one new strategic time-creating idea into your calendar (even one every two weeks is great progress).

Schedule a coffee every two weeks with another executive – particularly one who's a strong strategic thinker – to talk strategy and/or how to manage time more effectively in the organization (nothing gets you thinking strategically more than the need to prepare for regular strategic dialogue, particularly with a highly capable strategic thinker).

Remember, if you fail to make as much strategic time as you want or need, it's probably because you've neglected one or two elements in the strategic time model.

Make strategic thinking 'special'

I share dinner preparation duties with my wife. I notice that whenever I go into our kitchen around 5:30 p.m. to start dinner, I have a strong urge to drink wine – an urge I don't get when I enter any other room in the house or prepare any other meal (thank goodness). In fact, as I write this in my home office, I'm suddenly looking forward to making dinner tonight.

This happens because: a) when we bundle a less desirable task (making dinner) with a highly desirable one (red wine); and b) associate certain tasks with a specific environmental context, (kitchen at 5:30 p.m.), we're more likely to carry out the task.

For instance, the routine I use to do strategic thinking is almost always identical: I rise very early, slip out of the bedroom without waking my wife (using the same sequence of steps every morning). I go down the hall to my home office, restart my computer and turn on my desk lamp before descending the stairs to brew a coffee, drink a glass of water (with a vitamin D tablet) and make a one-minute check of sports scores, all before ascending the stairs and hitting my desk by 5:15 a.m.

My work is laid out beside my computer, phone and Outlook notifications are off, and all other work is out of sight (I've made sure to leave my desk that way the evening before so I can fall right into action). For me, there's something very enticing about reentering the pool of light made by my desk lamp and computer, coffee in hand, and diving right into my most strategic work. In fact, this routine is so special to me, I'm motivated to curtail alcohol intake and get to bed early the evening before so I 'hit the bricks' as ready as possible – when I abandon this simple routine, I do much less strategic thinking. I've repeated this routine so often that it feels like I've lost something significant in my life when I don't follow it.

My routine probably sounds horrible to you (after all, it's designed especially for me), so build one for yourself. It might be in your work office, at 11:00 a.m., in a specific meeting room, chair or desk that's reserved for strategic thinking. You might do operational work on your desk facing the door and do strategic work on the credenza with a view of the outside. My point – consciously build a routine and environment that makes strategic-thinking time uniquely special for you, and you're much more likely to seek it out.

Spend more time with strategic people and strategic information

When I was a kid, we'd visit our relatives in Cape Breton, Nova Scotia, for a couple of weeks each summer. My cousins had very strong accents – a careless blend of Irish and Scottish ancestry – and typically, by day three of our visit I would adopt their accents and become immersed in things important to them in their lives. I had similar experiences in university when summer jobs had me drive a truck or work in a warehouse. Both were new worlds I'd adapt to (almost) unconsciously.

This tendency to soak up the interests and behaviors of those around us is well established in research. In Chapter 9, I talked about the importance of an executive's First and Second Team – if you want to engage in more strategic thinking and dialogue, spend more time with your First Team and its members, especially those most strategically capable. Ask them about the strategic issues they face, schedule coffee or lunch to get their views on broader trends, disruption, etc. Use volunteer opportunities on your Chamber of Commerce and charitable boards to focus on strategic concerns and meet strategically capable people from outside your organization. Attend conferences that focus on strategic issues and trends and attract strategically minded people from across your industry.

Quality time with your Second Team (and other departmental/functional employees) is clearly important. Just know, the more time you spend there, the more likely you'll find yourself drifting into the weeds.

Of course, it's not just other people that influence our interests and behaviors. Our phone and its easy access to social media provides a direct channel to content that's potentially productive or a waste of brain cells. For instance, I enjoy political dialogue and used to find myself checking my favorite news sites whenever I had a free moment, such as waiting for a flight. The time these quick check-ins consumed over the course of a day was significant, however, it was my focus and attention that really suffered – two minutes taking in a video meant another three to four minutes (minimum) reflecting on what I'd seen. Over time, conversations with others started bleeding into political discourse – a potential source of useless discord if ever there was one. I found more and more of my time focused on something that lent zero strategic value to my life.

To counter this, I did two things: a) dropped access to all my favorite news sites except one; and b) changed my Twitter feed, replacing all political sources I followed with strategic sources – authors, thinkers, business people, etc., who share my interest in executive development. This simple switch was surprisingly easy to pull off with immediate benefits – less than five minutes a day wasted on news (it's surprising how informed you can be with this minimal commitment), my political discourse has virtually ended (my wife is delighted) and I'm taking in dozens of new ideas a day on subjects that directly feed my passion and career and stimulate strategic thinking.

Make the next 'X' great

The coach of a very successful NHL hockey team was talking about how he keeps his players motivated and focused over a long, grinding, 82-game season. First, he gets buy-in on a shared, overarching goal – make the playoffs. However, because that goal is too distant and abstract for most, he continuously breaks it down into smaller, more relatable goals.

For instance, he emphasizes a strong 20-game start to the season. In those 20 games, he stresses great play in the first three games. Within those first three games, he underlines their need to have nine 'good periods' (each game has three periods). Within each period, he asks them to commit to four or five great shifts.

That's a bit granular for me, however, I do find it helpful to continuously bring focus to my next week, knowing if I put together a series of great weeks, I'm likely to hit long-term allocations and objectives. On Sunday evenings, I get clear about: a) how I did in the previous week as it relates to strategic time; and b) what I'm trying to accomplish in the upcoming week and recommit to honoring the full strategic time model – maintain allocations, monitor regularly, look for opportunities to create time, and consistently consider time as a key organizational resource. This takes less than five minutes.

If my performance in the previous week hasn't been very good, I find this check-in galvanizes me to do better in the next week. If the last week has been great, it motivates me to maintain my performance. Regardless of the time frame you choose, begin it by forming a clear intention about how you want it to transpire and dive in.

Try a lot of things

I have stressed that the best way to extract value from this book and begin making strategic time is to take away one idea and put it into practice ASAP – no application in real life, no benefit. In addition, as much as possible, start with the easiest idea to implement. Nothing breeds success like success.

However, once you've done one thing, do another and another and another – keep applying different ideas. Use as many as you can, from small ideas like downloading a to-do-list app or dropping a meeting to larger ones like a 'meeting audit' in your department. The quantity of ideas you try is important because: a) some ideas won't work for you in your life, and you may have to try a bunch before finding the good ones; b) repeatedly applying time-making ideas builds your strategic time muscle; and c) the more ideas that do work, the more strategic time you create.

Timing is (almost) everything

If you're entering your busiest time of the year or there's some sort of unusual, short to mid-term pressure on your calendar, you might want to postpone the establishment of a new strategic time regimen until things clear up a bit. Instead, go to Chapter 8, deploy as many quick time-creating ideas as possible to relieve pressure, and explore the full strategic time model more fully when you've got a better chance for success. In addition, if you've established a solid regimen and hit a short to mid-term time crisis, scale back on strategic time as much as needed until you're over the hump – just make sure to give yourself a deadline for when things are to return to normal (and stick to it).

Do it for others

Remember the four diagrams from the section, 'Senior executives in the weeds drive everyone into the weeds' (Chapter 2)? Every time a CEO gets in the weeds, i.e. works at a level of problem difficulty lower than they should, they drive their senior executives there as well. They in turn drive the executives reporting to them into the weeds, and on it goes down through the department/function/organization.

As a boss, you're free to get into pretty much anything you want at every level in the organization, even if it's not good for you or anyone else. Are there things you can do to counter your worst intentions? Can you ask your direct reports to tell you when they see you drop into the weeds? Can you form an intention before meetings to elevate your thinking and the group's dialogue to higher-level problems? Can you meet with your boss once a month/quarter and ask whether they see you focused appropriately? Can you use your first coffee of the day to remind yourself to stay out of the weeds for the next 12 hours, for your own sake and everyone else's?

If/when you struggle and fail

As they say, 'If at first you don't succeed, try and try again.' I anticipate following the advice in this book will be challenging for many, so I've included a simple diagnostic that you can use to analyze why you're struggling or failing and hopefully get you back on track as soon as possible.

I recommend you follow the steps in the sequence I've provided. They come from a variety of sources, but follow a sequence laid out in the book *Analyzing Performance Problems.*[3]

---

10 STEPS FOR DIAGNOSING CONSISTENT FAILURE TO MAKE STRATEGIC TIME

1. NORMALIZE THE ISSUE
2. GET CLEAR ABOUT THE PROBLEM
3. IS THE PROBLEM WORTH SOLVING
4. HAVE YOU SET CLEAR ALLOCATIONS/EXPECTATIONS

5. ARE YOUR RESOURCES ADEQUATE
6. ARE YOU MONITORING YOUR PERFORMANCE
7. IS DESIRED PERFORMANCE PUNISHING
8. IS POOR PERFORMANCE REWARDING
9. IS BEHAVIOR APPROPRIATELY PUNISHED/REWARDED
10. DO YOU NEED TO BUILD CAPABILITY

Step 1 – normalize the issue

Normalization is a process by which we attempt to destigmatize behavior and alter our attitudes towards it, making it easier to develop the behavior we want.(4)

The attitude I want to confront (in case it exists) is that failure to make strategic time – even continuous failure – is some sign of a personal failing: a lack of ambition, a personality flaw, or some other immutable fact. The vast majority of executives are bright, conscientious people and most of the time, failure is an unintended consequence of perfectly natural circumstances (like the ones we discussed in Chapter 4) or the result of insufficient learning and development.

In other words, it's normal to struggle and fail when making strategic time. In fact, most of your colleagues are struggling with it right now (but they might be good at hiding it). It's very likely that with the advice in this book (or elsewhere) combined with practice, you'll be as successful as you want to be.

Step 2 – get clear about the problem

You've just checked your schedule and there's a gap between where your allocations say your time should be spent and where it's currently being spent. Is it a big gap or a small one? Is it a temporary gap or a persistent one? Is it an easy problem to address or is it going to take a big effort? Is the problem and solution obvious or does the underlying issue lie elsewhere?

The point here is to a) recognize there's a problem; and b) identify its real source. Go back to Chapter 4 and look at all the ways unintended consequences can push us into the weeds. For instance, there's little point in recalibrating your schedule if the source of the problem is misaligned performance expectations your boss and direct reports have about how you spend your time – any change to your schedule probably won't survive if you don't shift their misperceptions. So before moving to solution, pin down the real, underlying problem(s) and wrestle it/them to the ground. Write out, 'The real problem I must solve is X' and then build your solution.

Step 3 – is the problem worth solving?

If you're trying to make strategic time, you're likely asking yourself to change current behaviors you haven't previously exhibited as consistently as you'd like. As discussed in Chapter 4, the first step in behavioral change is forming a strong intention. Why is making strategic time so important to you? What are the benefits of making the change? Is it about better fulfilling your fiduciary role as an executive, saving your job, company or organization from the impact of disruption? Or is it a personal development opportunity and a better chance for promotion or fulfilled potential? Make sure you understand what is at stake regarding the change.

In addition, think about the consequences of not making the change. Most people focus on the benefits of change, but intention is stronger when you keep both: a) the benefits of change; and b) the consequences of not changing clearly in view. Draw a line on a piece of paper and list benefits on the left and consequences on the right.

Step 4 – have you set clear expectations/allocations?

Allocations are promises or expectations you have for yourself – they're a powerful behavioral guide. Amid distraction and overwhelm, they remind you of the behavior you need to exhibit, for example two hours of strategic time a day if you hope to reach big objectives and/or 30% of time on highest-level problems. As Lewis Carroll said, 'If you don't know where you're going any road will take you there.' But because you've carried out Step 3, you know why you want strategic time. Have you set clear time allocations that will get you there? Are they the right allocations or do they need to shift? Review your allocations periodically and re-clarify them if you must.

Step 5 – are your resources adequate?

Is the reason for your failure a lack of resources? Would an EA, a collaborative networking tool, email filters, better use of dictation, or a time-management application help? Have you designated a direct report or two (perhaps people you consider prime succession candidates for your own role when you're promoted) and properly trained them to take on a series of lower-level responsibilities you want to delegate? Achieving your goals may demand some time and/or financial investment on your part, and now's the time to better arm yourself with the resources that might support success.

Step 6 – are you monitoring your performance?

Your allocations tell you what 'good' looks like, but unless you're consistently tracking time and checking to see whether they're being honored, you won't know when and what's driving you into the weeds. Refer to Chapter 7 for tips on monitoring strategic time. It also pays to consider help from your boss or a colleague (another great advantage of a good EA) – anyone who can provide feedback on progress, offer advice, and help hold you accountable for your time allocations. If you haven't shared your aspirations with someone who can provide support and feedback, consider doing it now.

Step 7 – is desired performance punishing?

Let's say you've done a great job making appropriate time allocations and sticking to them. Congratulations. However, your commitment to strategic time is pulling focus away from other key responsibilities, i.e. important lower-level initiatives you're responsible for overseeing have slipped. As a result, you're taking heat and are tempted to drop some strategic time to patch things up. Before you do, consider other alternatives (there are always lots of alternatives) or, if absolutely necessary, make a very temporary adjustment with a hard deadline for reinstating your strategic time.

Step 8 – is poor performance rewarding?

You're not making any strategic time and it's OK. Life goes on as normal and reading this book was a waste of money and time. If that accurately describes your situation, I don't blame you for not changing. But are you sure life's going on as normal? Reread Chapters 1 and 2 – maybe the good times aren't here to stay, and you're feeling comfortable because you haven't made the strategic time needed to truly understand your situation (you're a traditional cab company about six months before Uber's launch). Your boss and your direct reports appear happy with things right now, but are you sure they're not looking for more strategic behavior and better management – have you specifically asked them? Reread Chapter 9 – are there significant personal and organizational improvements you can bring them (that they're not even aware of) by managing strategic time more effectively? Remember, 'What got you here won't get you there' – a lack of strategic time might be OK now, but what about six months from now? What about your next role – can your inability to make strategic time and/or think strategically survive another promotion? There may be countless personal and organizational incentives to ignore everything you've read in this book, just think very carefully about whether the status quo is really going to work for you in the long run.

Step 9 – is behavior appropriately punished/rewarded?

Executives and other high achievers tend to have very high standards for themselves. As soon as they accomplish something, they move past it like it's no big deal and refocus on the next challenge. However, when you (or others) don't recognize your accomplishments, it's easy to look back and see nothing standing out besides failures – no wonder so many executives suffer from some form of imposter syndrome.

This is one reason that I've recommended you have at least one organizationally sanctioned strategic initiative on your plate at all times. This ensures that your boss is aware of strategic successes and holding you accountable for failures.

If you don't have others who can appropriately administer rewards or consequences, do it yourself. For instance, if you successfully honor your time allocations for a quarter, take your partner out for a celebratory dinner. Conversely, if you fail to honor them, withhold a reward or normally pleasurable activity until your behavior changes. Remember, 'The road to hell is paved with good intentions.' Rewards and punishments work, so figure out how to use them to make strategic time.

Step 10 – do you need to build capability?

Have you taken action? Because without action there's only good intentions, and they're not enough to shift behavior – we all need practice to work ourselves through the four stages of the Conscious Competence Model to improved capability. If you haven't taken action, go to Chapter 8 and immediately institute the simplest, easiest time-creating idea. Then implement another one. If they don't work, try other alternatives. Consult others to see if something they're doing will work for you as well. Go back to Chapter 5 and reacquaint yourself with my simple strategic time model – success might simply be recommitment to all four elements because implementing two or three isn't getting the job done.

If nothing works – you can't make strategic time

Because so many executives struggle to make strategic time, at the end of the day we have to consider the option that some people simply don't make it because they can't. They just don't want to – they're perfectly happy working with lower-level problems or they can't seem to get it done no matter how much they try. I get it. If this was a book about knitting, there's no amount of intention and practice that's going to have me making my own sweaters.

However, I don't have a fiduciary responsibility to wear a hand-made cardigan, and executives do have a fiduciary obligation to develop and implement strategy as effectively as they can. And you can't do that without making strategic time. I have met many executives who decide the next level of problem difficulty isn't for them – they're happy to get very good at solving the problems they're facing at their level of the organization and leave highest-level problems to someone else. That's OK, as long as someone's working on them.

Conclusion

Building habits that consistently produce the strategic time you need is the surest way to get out (and stay out) of the weeds. However, even strong habits are susceptible to struggle and failure. If that happens to you, this chapter offers a simple diagnostic you can apply to yourself (or use with others to help them achieve success) that will identify the problem and hopefully get things back on track.

Topics we covered in Chapter 10 – Stimulate success and diagnose failure.

Topic	Page
• Introduction	171
• Getting started – make it habitual	171
• Don't boil the ocean – seek small, steady improvement	172
• Beware conscious incompetence	172
• Deploy a system that uses the whole strategic time model	173
• Make strategic thinking 'special'	174
• Spend more time with strategic people and strategic information	176
• Make the next 'X' great	177
• Try a lot of things	178
• Timing is (almost) everything	178
• Do it for others	178
• If/when you struggle and fail	179
• Step 1 – normalize the issue	180
• Step 2 – get clear about the problem	180
• Step 3 – is the problem worth solving?	181
• Step 4 – have you set clear expectations/allocations?	181
• Step 5 – are your resources adequate?	182
• Step 6 – are you monitoring your performance?	182
• Step 7 – is desired performance punishing?	182
• Step 8 – is poor performance rewarding?	183
• Step 9 – is behavior appropriately punished/rewarded?	183
• Step 10 – do you need to build capability?	184
• If nothing works – you can't make strategic time	184
• Conclusion	185

11 CONCLUSION

IN MANY WAYS, this book is a validation of everything I've presented here. Writing it was a key strategic objective of mine that I added to my normal client workload, and I couldn't have done it without sticking to my strategic time allocations, monitoring progress, instituting a host of time-creating tools/techniques (the Pomodoro technique, dictation, and a to-do-list app stand out as lifesavers), and managing my time effectively.

I hope you've enjoyed reading this book and applying some of the ideas as much as I've enjoyed writing it. I've seen these ideas work for many executives and executive teams, and I'm confident they'll work for you.

More than anything, I hope it prompts you to get more serious about your responsibility to make strategic time and helps you fulfill that responsibility more effectively. Strategic time is time dedicated to strategic priorities, the priorities that create maximum organizational and personal value – time that's most meaningful. I want you to have as much of it as you need, and we'll all benefit from the results.

If you want to learn more about improving the effectiveness of individual executives and executive teams - including additional information on how to make strategic time - you can find articles, tools, and techniques on the subject (including a weekly blog) at SeniorTeamAdvisory.com.

THANK YOU

There are a number of people I'd like to thank for their guidance, help, and support. I couldn't have written this book without them. In alphabetical order, they are Wayne Boyle, Peter Brown, Anne Cogdon, Xavier Comas, Derek Dempster, Steve Foran, Bjorn Gunderson, Stephen Harrington, Fiona Kirkpatrick Parsons, Alaina Lavoie, Nancy MacKay (and MacKay CEO Forums), Greg MacQuarrie, Mike Marsh, Barbara Meens-Thistle, Rob Myatt, Jenny O'Donnell, Alex Twells, Calvin Simpson (and others at Happful), Shannon Sumarah, and Kathy Woods. In addition, a huge thanks to Deloitte and all my wonderful clients for years of enjoyable, enriching work together.

Having said that, I have to single out my wife Anne Cogdon for a contribution that always – in every facet of our life together – goes way beyond the call of duty. She's amazing.

REFERENCES

Chapter 1 – Is there a problem?

1. Corporate Decision-Making: Why Do Large, Once-Successful Companies Fail? Gary Cokins, 2012.
2. Built to Change: How to Achieve Sustained Organizational Effectiveness, Edward E. Lawler, Christopher Worley and Jerry Porras, 2006.
3. Global Survey: Hyper Disruption and Digitization Leading Forces of Change Within Business, 2019 Universe Research Teradata (survey conducted by Vanson Bourne), 2019.
4. C-Suite Challenge 2019, The Conference Board, 2018.
5. Allianz Risk Barometer 2019: Cyber Joins Business Interruption as a Leading Global Risk for Companies for First Time, 2019.
6. CEO's Curbed Confidence Spells Caution, PwC's 22nd Annual Global CEO Survey, 2019.
7. The Biggest Obstacles to Innovation in Large Companies, Scott Kirsner, Harvard Business Review, 2018.
8. The Three Challenges Every CEO Faces, Neal H. Kissel and Patrick Foley, Harvard Business Review, 2019.
9. The Law of Accelerating Returns, Ray Kurzweil, Accelerating Intelligence, 2001.

10. The Future of Employment: How Susceptible are Jobs to Computerization?, Carl Benedikt Frey and Michael A. Osborne, 2013.
11. The Future of Jobs Report, World Economic Forum, 2018.
12. Forces of Change: The Future of Health, Deloitte Insights, 2019.
13. 5 Surprising Numbers from Uber's Driver Data Report, Fortune Magazine, Laura Lorenzetti, January 2015.
14. Organization Strategy, Structure and Process, Raymond E. Miles and Charles C. Snow, 1978.
15. Age of Disruption: Are Canadian Firms Prepared? Deloitte's Future of Canada Series.

Chapter 2 – Who is responsible for organizational struggle and failure?

1. State of the American Manager: Analytics and Advice for Leaders, Gallup.
2. The Effective Executive, Peter F. Drucker, 1985.
3. Stop Wasting Valuable Time, Michael Mankins, Harvard Business Review, 2004.
4. Strategic Time Survey, Vince Marsh, 2019.
5. Making Time Management the Organization's Priority, McKinsey Quarterly, January, 2013.
6. If Strategy is So Important, Why Don't We Make Time For It, Dorie Clark, Harvard Business Review, 2018.
7. The Strategic Thinking Manifesto, Rich Horwath.
8. Bridges Business Consultancy Int., Strategy Implementation Survey Findings, 2012.
9. The Office of Strategy Management, Harvard Business Review, R.S. Kaplan and D.P. Norton, 2005.
10. Experiences That Develop the Ability to Think Strategically, Ellen Goldman, Terrence Cahill, Rubens Filho, and Laurence Merlis, Journal of Healthcare Management 54 no. 6, 2009:406.
11. Executives Fail to Execute Strategy Because They're Too Internally Focused,

Ron Carucci, HBR, November 2017.

12. CEO Turnover at Record High; Successors Following Long-Serving CEO's Struggling According to PwC's Strategy & Global Study, PwC, May 2019.
13. Successfully Transitioning to New Leadership Roles, McKinsey & Company, May 2018.
14. Turnover at the Top: Executive Team Departures and Firm Performance, James Guthrie and Jay Lee, Organization Science, June 2014.

Chapter 3 – Why do executives struggle and fail?

1. Improving Employee Engagement: A Solution for Leaders, Stephen F. Young and Michael D. Smith, Centre for Creative Leadership, September 2018.
2. State of the American Workplace Report: Five Ways to Improve Employee Engagement Now, Gallup, January 2014.
3. Strategic Leadership: Theory and Research on Executives, Top Management Teams and Boards, Finkelstein, Hambrick and Cannella Jr., 2009.
4. Groups Perform Better Than the Best Individuals at Solving Complex Problems, Journal of Personality and Social Psychology, American Psychological Association, 2006.
5. High Output Management, Andrew S. Grove, 1983.
6. Wicked Problems, Reductive Tendency and the Formation of (Non) Opportunity Beliefs, David Gras, Michael Conger, Anna Jenkins and Michael Gras, Journal of Business Venturing, September 2019.
7. College Students' Time Management: Correlations with Academic Performance and Stress, Therese H. Macan, Comila Shahani, Robert L. Dipboye, Amanda P. Phillips, Journal of Educational Psychology, 1990.

Chapter 4 – What prevents executives from making and maintaining strategic time?

1. How Hard Do Executives Really Work? Laura Vanderkam, October 2012.
2. The Leader's Calendar: How CEO's Manage Time, Michael Porter and Nitin Nohria, Harvard Business Review, 2018.
3. Your Scarcest Resource, Michael Mankins, Chris Brahm and Greg Caimi, May 2014.

4. A Detailed Study of CEO Habits Found that Leaders Spend 24 Percent of Their Time Checking Email – and Why it's Not Always Productive, Myelle Lansat, Business Insider, June 2018.

5. Most CEOs Read a Book a Week: This is How You Can Too, Brian D. Evans, Inc., June 2017.

6. A CEO's Guide to Talent Management Today, Vikram Bhalla, Jean-Michel Caye, Deborah Lovich and Peter Tollman, Boston Consulting Group, April 2018.

7. Do Managers Spend Too Much Time on Poor Performers at the Risk of Top Talent?, Jan Johnston Osburn, LinkedIn, August 2014.

8. Making Strategic Thinking Part of Your Job, Ron Carucci, Harvard Business Review, October 2016.

9. Deloitte's Leadership Development Practice, Assessment Data, 2019

10. Make Time for Work that Matters, Julia Birkinshaw and Jordan Cohen, September 2013.

11. Hogan Development Survey, Hogan Assessment Systems Inc., 1997.

12. Upper Echelons: The Organization as a Reflection of its Top Managers, Donald Hambrick and Phyllis Mason, Academy of Management Review, 1984.

13. Pew Research Centre, taken from Enlightenment Now, Stephen Pinker, 2015.

14. Impact of Team Performance Survey Report, ThinkWise, 2019.

15. Bridges Business Consultancy Int., Strategy Implementation Survey Findings, 2012.

16. Why Strategy Execution Unravels and What To Do About It, Donald Sull, Rebecca Homes and Charles Sull, Harvard Business Review, March 2015.

17. What CEOs Are Afraid Of, Roger Jones, Harvard Business Review, February 2015.

18. Deloitte's Leadership Development Practice, Assessment Data, 2019.

19. Assuming Leadership: The First 100 Days, Boston Consulting Group, 2003.

20. Taken from the podcast produced by Greylock Partners, *The Strategy of Blitzscaling* with Reid Hoffman and Chris Yeh, 2019.

21. Doodle, The State of Meetings Report, 2019.

Chapter 5 – How do executives effectively make and maintain strategic time?

1. Mental Models: How to Train Your Brain to Think in New Ways, James Clear, jamesclear.com/Feynman-mental-models.

Chapter 6 – Allocate strategic time – spot the high ground

1. Why 80 Percent of New Year's Resolutions Fail, Luciani, J., 2015.
2. Peter Drucker, The Effective Executive, 2002.
3. Make Time for the Work that Matters, Julien Birkenshaw and Jordan Cohen, HBR, September 2013.
4. 5 Reasons Why Writing Down Goals Increases the Odds of Achieving Them, Damian Pros, Elite Daily, June 2015.
5. Social Power and the CEO – Leadership and Trust in a Sustainable Free Enterprise System, Elliott Jaques, 2002.
6. Organization Strategy, Structure and Process, Raymond E. Miles and Charles C. Snow, 2003.
7. The Pomodoro Technique, Francesco Cirillo, 2013.
8. Brief and Rare Mental 'Breaks' Keep You Focused: Deactivation and Reactivation of Task Goals Preempt Vigilance Decrements, Atsunori Ariga, Alejandro Lleras, *Cognition*, 2011.
9. Jim Collins, Interview with Tim Ferris, The Tim Ferris Show, February 2019.
10. Managing Your Time as a Leader, Reflections: The SoL Journal on Knowledge, Learning and Change, Volume 7 Number 4.
11. Creativity and Constraints: Exploring the Role of Constraints in the Creative Processes of Research and Development Teams, Brent D. Rosso, Organization Studies, March 2014.
12. A Nobel Prize-winning Psychologist Explains Why We're Always Wrong About How Long Tasks Take, Corinne Purtill, (from Thinking, Fast and Slow, Daniel Kahneman), January 2019.

Chapter 7 – Monitor strategic time – get the lay of the land

1. Peter Drucker, The Effective Executive, 2002.
2. Workers are Bad at Filling Out Timesheets and it Costs Billions a Day, Gretchen Gavett, HBR, January 2015.
3. KPMG to Fine Staff 100 Pounds for Late Time Sheets, The Guardian, December 2018.
4. Time is Money: A Revealing Study Into the Cost of Today's Poor Time Tracking Habits & Technology, Accelo.
5. Stop the Meeting Madness, Leslie A. Perlow, Constance Noonan Hadley and Eunic Eun, HBR, July-August 2017.
6. Meetings Matter: Effects of Team Meetings on Team and Organizational Success, Simone Kauffeld and Nale Hehmann-Willenbrock, 2012.
7. The Four Player Model, David Kantor, Kantor Institute.

Chapter 8 – Create strategic time – pull weeds

1. Hogan Development Survey, Hogan Assessment Systems Inc., 1997.
2. Deloitte's Leadership Development Practice, Assessment Data, 2019.
3. Managers Must Delegate Effectively to Develop Employees, Sam R. Lloyd, Success Systems, 2012.
4. Stop Wasting Valuable Time, Michael Mankins, Harvard Business Review, September 2004.
5. How Much Time Do We Spend in Meetings, Martin, Cleverism, April 2019.
6. Why Email is Addictive and How to Break the Habit, Ashley Coolman, Productivity, November 2015.
7. Your Scarcest Resource, Michael Mankins, Chris Brahm and Greg Caimi, May 2014.
8. Bottom-up and Top-Down Attention are Independent, Yair Pinto, Andries R. van der Leij, Ilia G. Sligte, Victor A.F. Lamme, H. Steven Scholte, Journal of Vision, July 2013.
9. The Cost of Continuously Checking Email, Ron Friedman, Harvard Business Review, July 2014.

10. The Social Economy: Unlocking Value and Productivity Through Social Technologies, McKinsey Global Institute, July 2012.

Chapter 9 – Manage time – prevent weed growth

1. Upper Echelons: The Organization as a Reflection of its Top Managers, Donald Hambrick and Phyllis Mason, The Academy of Management Review, 1984.
2. The Hard Evidence: Business is Slowing Down, Tom Monahan, Fortune, January 2016.
3. Smart Rules: Six Ways to Get People to Solve Problems Without You, Yves Morieux, Boston Consulting Group, 2011.
4. Lack of Candor in Organizations, Conflict Dynamics Profile, a Network Associate of the Center for Creative Leadership.
5. The How of Transformation, Michael Bucy, Adrian Finlayson, Greg Kelly, and Chris Moye, McKinsey & Company, May 2016.
6. Deloitte Leadership Development Practice, 2019.
7. How Transition Programs Accelerate Executive Onboarding and Integration, Michael D. Watkins, IMD Research and Knowledge, June 2018.
8. Flipping the Odds for Successful Reorganization, Boston Consulting Group, April 2012.
9. Overcoming the Abysmal Reorganizing and Restructuring Failure Rates, The Clemmer Group.
10. Driving the Strategic Agenda in the New Work Environment, CEB, 2015.
11. The Collaborative Operating System, www.thecos.org.
12. Collaborative Overload, Rob Cross, Reb Rebele and Adam Grant, HBR, 2016.
13. Collaboration Overload is a Symptom of a Deeper Organizational Problem, Michael Mankins, HBR, March 2017.
14. Your Scarcest Resource, Michael Mankins, Chris Brahm and Greg Caimi, May 2014.
15. Money and Trust Among Strangers, Gabriele Camera, Marco Casari and Maria Bigoni, Proceedings of the National Academy of Sciences, August 2013.

16. How Much Time Do We Spend in Meetings? Hint: It's Scary, Martin, cleverism.com/time-spent-in-meetings.
17. Time, Talent, Energy: Overcome Organizational Drag & Unleash Your Team's Productive Potential, Michael Mankins and Eric Garton, Bain & Company, 2017.
18. How Meetings Kill Productivity, Ray Williams, Financial Post, April 2012.
19. Survey: Managers Spend 26% of Their Time Coaching Bad Employees, Jane Burnett, May 2018. (Taken from research by Robert Half: Staffing Agencies and Hiring Solutions.)
20. The Emperor's New Clothes: Confronting the Illusion of High-Performing Senior Teams, Vincent Marsh and Phil Sandahl, 2011.
21. State of Teams: White Paper for the Centre for Creative Leadership, Andre Martin and Vidula Bal, 2015.
22. The 5 Dysfunctions of a Team, Patrick Lencioni, 2002.
23. An Exploratory Study of Employee Silence: Issues that Employees Don't Communicate Upward and Why?, Francis J. Milliken, Elizabeth W. Morrison, Patricia F. Hewlin, November 2003.
24. How Inefficient Processes Waste Nearly a Third of Employees' Time, Adam Reynolds, Financial Director website, June, 2019.

Chapter 10 – Diagnose failure and get back on track

1. Atomic Habits: An Easy and Proven Way to Build Good Habits and Break Bad Ones, James Clear, 2018.
2. How are Habits Formed: Modelling Habit Formation in the Real World, Phillippa Lally, Cornelia H.M. van Jaarsveld, Henry W.W. Potts and Jane Wardle, 2009.
3. Analyzing Performance Problems, Robert F. Mager and Peter Pipe, 2012.
4. The Normalization Principle and its Human Management Implications, Bengt Nirje, 2009.

Made in the USA
Columbia, SC
13 April 2021

36097457R00115